The Automatic Pistol

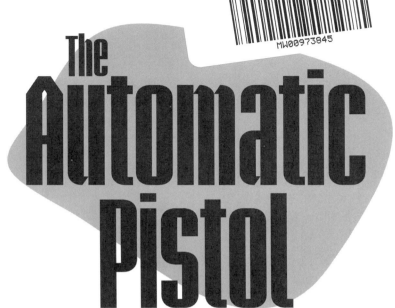

The Automatic Pistol
by J.B.L. Noel

Reprint edition 2004
Original publication 1919
Foreword copyright © 2004 by Timothy J. Mullin

ISBN 1-58160-462-9
Printed in the United States of America

Published by Paladin Press, a division of
Paladin Enterprises, Inc.
Gunbarrel Tech Center
7077 Winchester Circle
Boulder, Colorado 80301 USA
+1.303.443.7250

Direct inquiries and/or orders to the above address.

PALADIN, PALADIN PRESS, and the "horse head" design
are trademarks belonging to Paladin Enterprises and
registered in United States Patent and Trademark Office.

Visit our Web site at: www.paladin-press.com

The Automatic Pistol

J.B.L. NOEL
Fellow of the Royal Geographical Society

Foreword by
Timothy J. Mullin

PALADIN PRESS • BOULDER, COLORADO

ELEY
CARTRIDGES

In Peace or in War always
THE BEST

 6·35 m/m. or ·25" Automatic
(for Webley, Colt, Browning,
etc., Pistols).

 ·32" or 7·65 m/m. Automatic
(for Webley, Colt, Browning,
etc., Pistols).

 9 m/m. Automatic (for Webley
and Browning Pistols).

 ·38" Automatic (for Webley
and Colt Pistols)·

 ·45" Colt Automatic.

**To be obtained from all Gunmakers
and Registered Dealers in Ammunition.**

Wholesale only :—
ELEY BROTHERS, LTD.,
LONDON (ENGLAND).

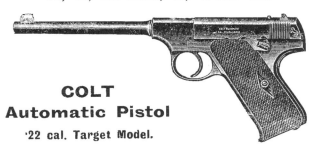

WEBLEY & SCOTT, Ltd.

Manufacturers of Revolvers, Automatic Pistols and All Kinds of High-Class Sporting Guns and Rifles.

CONTRACTORS TO HIS MAJESTY'S NAVY, ARMY, INDIAN AND COLONIAL FORCES.

"W.S." Bisley Target Revolver.

The Webley & Scott Target Revolvers achieved sweeping successes at Bisley, 70% of highest possibles having been made with these revolvers.

AUTOMATIC PISTOLS
.32 or 7.65 Calibre.

. 25 or 6.35 Calibre.

Waistcoat-Pocket Model.

ADVANTAGES OF WEBLEY AUTOMATICS.

No Tools required for dismounting.
Can be used as a Single Loader, Magazine being reserved for emergency.
Double Security Lock
Greater Smashing and Stopping Power than any other Automatic on the Market
Greater Accuracy at Long Ranges.
Solidity, Accuracy, Durability, Reliability Simplicity and Efficiency.

To be obtained from all **GUN DEALERS** and **WHOLESALE** at
Weamen St., Birmingham, & 78 Shaftesbury Avenue, London, W.

THE
AUTOMATIC PISTOL

BY

J. B. L. NOEL, F.R.G.S.

AUTHOR OF

" HOW TO SHOOT WITH A REVOLVER. "

London:
FORSTER GROOM & Co., Ltd., 15, Charing Cross. S.W. 1.
1919.

AUTHOR'S NOTE.

In order to promote interest in pistol shooting, particularly shooting for self-defence, the Author will be glad to correspond with readers (sending an addressed and stamped envelope) and reply to enquiries giving the best help and advice he can.

All people interested in pistol shooting
------ should obtain the following ------

THE MODERN PISTOL AND HOW TO SHOOT IT.
12/6 net.

AUTOMATIC PISTOL SHOOTING.
5/– net.

Both by the world-famous expert
MR. WALLER WINANS.

Other books are   .   .

THE BOOK OF THE PISTOL AND REVOLVER.
By H. POLLARD.   **10/6** net.

THE SERVICE REVOLVER AND HOW TO USE IT.
By CAPTAIN C. D. TRACEY.   **3/–** net.

CONTENTS.

———

FOREWORD

John Baptist Lucius Noel was an English officer and acknowledged handgun shooting expert. He was a follower of that most talented of expatriate Americans, Walter Winans, who despite being a superb target man was also a very practical shooter. Noel went with the British army to France during World War I and soon understood that for the type of fighting that was occurring there, the handgun was one of the finest possible fighting instruments. But most people then, as now, really did not understand how to use it as a fighting tool.

Noel set out to learn how to effectively use it, train his troops in its use, and ultimately teach the entire British army how to use the handgun as a practical fighting tool. He sought to teach the British soldier how to use the handgun as an offensive weapon—not merely as a badge of office or even a defensive tool for the officer or soldier who could not utilize a rifle.

Who exactly was John Noel, the author of this little jewel? How did he come to write this book? What became of him? Did he write anything else of equal benefit to today's gunfighter?

Born on February 26, 1890, at Newton Abbott, Devon, England, John Baptist Lucius Noel was the grandson of the second Earl of Gainsborough. He attended art school in Florence, Italy, for a period, but his only formal education took place in Switzerland, where he sat at the back of the class for the 2 1/2 years he attended. While he may not have been much of a student in Switzerland, it was there that he began to develop his lifelong love of mountaineering.

Noel's father was a lieutenant colonel in the Rifle Brigade, and he encouraged his son to follow a military career. In 1909 Noel was commissioned in the East Yorkshire Regiment out of Sandhurst, and he spent five years in India with his regiment. While stationed in Calcutta, he decided to make an attempt at climbing in the Everest region. Though Tibet was closed to foreigners, Noel apparently had a flair for language and disguise and in 1913 managed to get within 40 miles of the famed mountain while disguised as a Mohammedan from India. He was taken prisoner by the Tibetan authorities after some gunplay but managed to talk his way out and was allowed to leave.

When World War I started in 1914, Noel was at home on leave in England and joined as a lieutenant in the King's Own Yorkshire Light Infantry, his own regiment still being in India. He was involved in actions at Mons, Le Cateau, Ypres, and Hill 60. Taken prisoner by the Germans, he managed to escape back to British lines and, after a period in the hospital, rejoined his unit. He was promoted to captain and served in Ypres in 1915.

By 1917 he was appointed acting major and assigned to the Machine Gun Corps (a separate branch at the time) and in that capacity was made responsible for revolver training. Obviously such training was very important for members of this branch, as the weight involved in handling the machine guns, ammo, and accessories ruled out carrying a rifle for self-defense.

Noel wrote this manual in his capacity as revolver training officer for the Machine Gun Corps. He noted that while written for soldiers, it was useful for travelers and others who needed or used the revolver. Throughout his course of training, the emphasis was on quick shooting at close quarters—war work, not a formal course of fire that existed prior to that time. Training covered the proper use of the revolver for quick shooting at running targets and appearing, disappearing, and advancing targets. Teaching the student to understand the nature of the handgun was half the battle; teaching the student to use it quickly at ranges of 5 feet to 30 yards, mostly within 5–15 feet was the rest. Noel thought six hits on a man target at 15 yards in 12 seconds was fair shooting and the same in three seconds made a person a crack shot. Shooting speed was critically important, and within the limits of a man target, faster was better than smaller. Given the use intended, the sights of the period, and the typical nighttime use of the weapon in trench raids, it is not surprising that Noel preferred teaching the student to shoot by sense of direction and instinct.

Noel believed that "pistol shooting . . . should be one of the recognized pillars of every man's education." (One wonders what he would think of today's England with its handgun bans. Perhaps he would not be surprised at the consequences of such policies.) He wrote *How to Shoot with a Revolver* in 1918 and published this book one year later.

In 1921, Noel became the revolver instructor at the newly developed Small Arms School at Hythe, and his theories were constantly taught and referenced in the postwar era.

Always something of a mountaineer, Noel was a member of two British expeditions to climb Mount Everest—one in 1922 and the other the ill-fated 1924 expedition in which George Mallory and Andrew Irvine were killed as they attempted to reach the summit. Noel acted as the official photographer for these expeditions, taking both motion pictures and stills, and proved himself a true pioneer in this art. During the inter-war period he went on many lecture tours in England and the United States to speak about his Everest expeditions, and he has been referred to as perhaps the most successful mountaineering lecturer of all times.

During World War II, Noel revised his manual and re-released it without any major changes, his theories and practices having been confirmed to be useful many times over. He served as a staff intelligence officer in the Far East, and his photography from the air was one of the main reasons the military chose the Stillwell Road supply route from India to Burma. After the war, he retired to Kent in England and became an expert in the restoration of old Kentish homes. It does appear that he thought about revising his gun books of the World War I period, as notes from the time he was in his 80s and early 90s survive to show an interest in the subject. More the pity that it did not get done.

Noel died in 1989 shortly after his 99th birthday; he was one of the last surviving officers of the original British Expeditionary Force of 1914.

While among mountaineers he was known as a famed climber, gun people recognize him as one of the greatest practitioners in the effective use of the modern handgun. The significance of this book is that it reflects the thoughts, theories, and experiences of a man who had both used his methods in the no-man's land of France and seen his teachings used by thousands more. When you read his words, you will get to experience the lessons taught and learned, tried and found successful by men long gone "west," as would have been said in 1918. You have some valuable lessons to be learned in the pages ahead and valuable experiences to gain.

Timothy J. Mullin
St. Louis, Missouri
July 2004

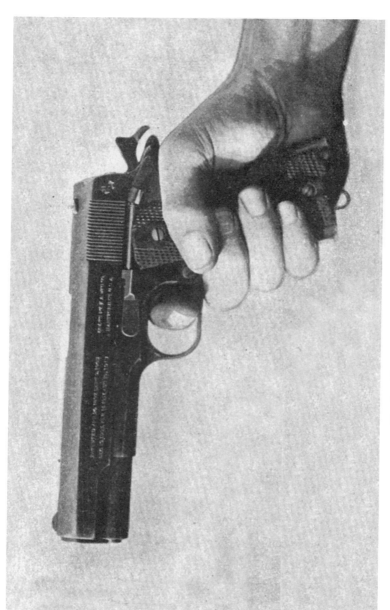

Fig. 1.—The Grip on a .45 Colt Automatic.

CHAPTER I.

PISTOL SHOOTING.

Pistol shooting is a subject which is avoided and mistrusted by the generality of people; but those who take up its practice at once become fascinated by it, and fully appreciate its practical value.

Pistol shooting should be made a national pastime. Shooting clubs are a far more healthy and intellectual form of public amusement than the sordid and effeminate amusements of cheap theatres and dancing saloons so prevalent in our towns. Pistol shooting and horse riding should be one of the recognised pillars of every man's education.

The aim of this little book is to outline the principles of pistol shooting, and describe clearly and simply the method of learning to shoot. Thus, to commence with, we will study the characteristics of the automatic, in order to see what principles govern its use.

The pistol is a one-handed weapon, used without support to the hand or arm; so this, combined with, the short distance between the sights, makes it a weapon unsuitable for taking a steady, deliberate aim. In this way it differs from a rifle, which is supported steadily, by two hands, and which has a long distance between the sights. Many people do not realise this essential difference; and they apply the same method of aiming—the deliberate aim—to the pistol as they do to the rifle. With a pistol there should be no dwelling on the aim. The aim

2

and trigger release are simultaneous and instinctive. The trigger is released *while the pistol is in motion.*

Furthermore, the pistol, being a one-handed weapon with a short barrel, has the advantage of being quick to align on the target. You can get into action either from the ready position, pistol in the hand, or from the unready position, pistol in the holster, quicker than you can with a long-barrelled rifle. Again, you can shoot in any direction, to the front, to the sides and behind you. You can conceal a pistol, and suddenly shoot unawares. All these characteristics make the pistol a weapon of opportunity and a weapon for quick shooting.

One may summarise by saying that a rifle is a weapon for deliberate shooting at long range against stationary or slowly moving targets. The pistol is a weapon for quick shooting at close quarters against moving targets. Owing to this difference, the method of firing with the pistol is essentially different from that with the rifle.

We see now that the guiding consideration must be to learn and practise quick shooting. You cannot claim to be a pistol shot unless you are a, quick shot.

The author wishes to emphasise this point particularly, because so many. people have quite the wrong idea, practising only slow shooting at bull's-eye stationary targets. The test of shooting should not be the smallness of the group of shots placed on a stationary target, but rather the rapidity with which a hit or a succession of hits can be thrown on a target representing the silhouette of a man. For this reason, in this little book, only quick shooting is discussed. The pistol must be used on all occasions according to its characteristics—a weapon for quick shooting.

We will now go on to see the method of learning to shoot. The fundamental principles can be explained simply as these:—

The first stage is—
Accuracy.—Depending on
    1. Correct grip;
    2. Developing sense of direction;
    3. The art of trigger pressing.

The second stage is—
The Development of rapidity and shooting by sense of direction.

Correct Grip.

We will take each of these in turn and see first of all correct grip.

In pistol shooting you try to approximate the action of throwing from the hand; and the basis of all practice is to use this natural power of pointing of the hand.

Suppose you pointed with your forefinger at any object in front of you, you would find that your eye guided your hand in pointing. So also your eye must guide your bullet.

The object of correct grip is to hold the pistol in the hand in such a way that when the pistol is quickly pointed at any mark the sights come naturally into the

Fig. 2.

Aiming mark with black vertical line beneath for practising snapshooting and rapid firing. Diameter of mark 3/4". Firer stands 12 feet away.

The line assists in practising the quick alignment of sights up to the mark.

line of sight of the eye to the mark. Holding in this way, called "correct grip," thus enables you to shoot instinctively; and your bullet would go straight to the mark, even if you did not look along the sights, but kept your eyes fixed on the mark.

Take the pistol in the hand, and, holding it at arm's length pointing to the ground in front, direct the eyes to a mark, and raise the pistol straight to the mark. Notice whether the sights come straight up into the line of sight. Adjust your hand on the butt until you get this grip correct.

To get the sights in line laterally will depend upon how far the hand is round the butt, gauged by the relative positions of the knuckles and trigger guard. Getting the sights to rise level, horizontally correct, will depend upon the height of the hand on the butt. The higher the hand, the higher the foresight rises. As a general rule the hand must be held up as high as possible; but it must be recognised that no definite rule can be laid down for the position of the hand. Whatever grip gives you the natural alignment of the sights will be *your* correct grip. You must test and find this out for your own hand and pistol.

A grave defect with some pistols is that they have the butts placed at right angles to the line of the barrel; and this (see figure 15) causes the sights to point low when the wrist is held naturally. The wrist has to be bent up, which is a disadvantage. However, manufacturers are realising this defect, and are remedying it now by fitting improved sloping butts, such as those of the ·45 Colt Government Model and the ·22 Colt Target Automatic.

Developing sense of direction.

This is developing the natural power of pointing of the hand called sense of direction, and so accustoming the hand and arm to the weight and balance of the pistol that the sights can be rapidly and accurately aligned in any direction, on any mark, upon which the eye is fixed.

Try the experiment of raising the pistol quickly to different marks in turn, and you will see that you lack the power of bringing the sights straight, dead to the mark. Often you will miss the mark or fail to find the sights. Your arm will quickly tire at the shoulder.

This development of the muscles and cooperation between the eye and the arm, resulting in quick alignment of the pistol, is got by special muscle exercises that will be explained later.

The art of Trigger Pressing.

The art of shooting with firearms lies almost wholly in the trigger release. With the pistol, because it is a single-handed weapon, used without support to the hand or arm, trigger pressing will be even more important than with the rifle. The slightest error in trigger pressing, either by jerking or by lateral pulling, will cause exaggerated errors in firing.

Every bad shot can almost invariably be attributed to faulty trigger pressing.

The first thing to learn is to squeeze the trigger—to release it by a tightening squeeze of the *whole* hand, and not by an independent jerk of the trigger finger.

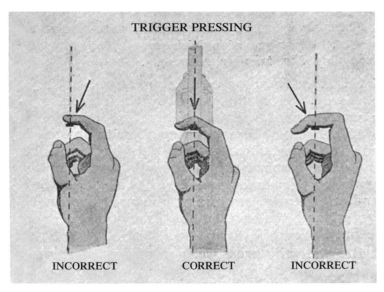

TRIGGER PRESSING

INCORRECT   CORRECT   INCORRECT

Fig. 3.—Exerting the trigger pressure along the line of
the axis of the barrel.

Take your pistol in your hand and hold it at the hip,
close to your body. Cock the hammer, and practise
releasing the trigger by a squeeze of the whole hand, as
if you were pressing water out of a sponge. You should
feel the trigger sliding through. Go on practising this
until you train your hand automatically to take this uniform tightening squeeze. Unless you train yourself to do
this automatically you will forget to do it when firing;
and you will pull your trigger by a jerk or independent
action of the forefinger, which will result in a bad shot.

The pressure of the finger must be exerted in the
line of the axis of the barrel. Pressing on the left or

right of the trigger will deflect the shot laterally. These mistakes will be readily seen when shooting at a target on the range.

After learning the correct way to press the trigger, the next step will be to practise the *timing of the trigger release.*

Stand in front of an aiming mark, about 12 feet away. Hold the pistol by the correct grip, hammer cocked, pistol pointing to the ground at 45 degrees. Direct the eyes on to the mark, and lift the pistol straight to the mark. As the arm rises commence the trigger pressing by tightening gradually the grip with the whole hand, the forefinger taking the pressure on the trigger, and the rest of the hand tightening on the butt.

Regulate the pressure, according to the speed of raising the pistol, in such a way that the final pressure necessary to release the trigger is exerted just at the moment the sights come aligned on the mark.

This timing of the trigger release needs more practice than anything else in pistol shooting. The more you shoot the more you will realise that *the whole art of shooting lies in trigger pressing.*

Anybody, provided they have a steady arm, can align the sights on the mark, but why can't they throw the bullet on the mark? Simply because they jerk it off by bad trigger pressing.

The advantage of this method is that you get slow trigger pressing, although you are shooting quickly, because the trigger pressing commences at the moment you start to lift the arm. It is completed by the time you have lifted the arm. By the method of deliberate aiming, on the contrary, the trigger pressing commences *after* the sights are aligned. Therefore, in the first place, it is late, resulting in waste of time, and secondly it is hurried, resulting in bad shooting.

The trigger pull should not be above 5lbs. About 3lbs. is a good mean between the accuracy of the hair trigger and the safety of the heavy pull. But no definite rule can be laid down, because this will depend upon the individual and the strength of his hand.

Second stage of training.
The development of rapidity, and shooting by sense of direction.

Proficiency in rapid shooting depends upon the three foregoing stages of training—correct grip, developing sense of direction, and correct trigger release ALL COMBINED TOGETHER.

There is no hanging on the aim; but the trigger is squeezed the moment the sights become aligned, as the pistol is raised to the mark from underneath.

There is no limit to speed. First of all you practise firing raising the pistol slowly. Later, with training, you can aim and fire as fast as you can raise the pistol to the mark.

At very close quarters and for very quick shooting the sights may often by dispensed with, and training in correct grip and sense of direction be depended upon to align the pistol instinctively to the mark, although the sights may not be used. This is called shooting by sense of direction.

Fig. 4.—The .45 Colt (U.S. Government model).

Chapter II.

LEARNING TO BE SAFE WITH A PISTOL.

"The short barrel makes the pistol portable and handy, and enables a rapid change of target to be made." This characteristic, which makes the pistol such a useful weapon for fighting, at the same time makes it a dangerous weapon to use. With the same ease with which it can be swung round to hit targets appearing at the front, sides, and back of you, so it is equally easy to point the pistol, inadvertently, at yourself or your friends.

You can become safe with a pistol only by learning its correct handling so thoroughly that it becomes a second nature to you. In using a pistol in an emergency, when timid or excited, you will forget all safety rules which you observed while shooting on the range. If, however, you handle your pistol correctly on every occasion when carrying it, practising with it, and firing with it you will find that correct handling becomes instinctive; and so you will always be safe, although at times your attention may be completely diverted from what you are doing.

The first habit to learn is—
　　To prove your pistol every time you draw it from the holster;
　　Never hand over or accept a pistol unless proved.

It is easy to distinguish the man who is disciplined and experienced, because you will see him proving his pistol every time he draws it from the holster; every time he picks it up to practise with or to shoot with; every time he hands it to somebody else. Get into the habit of doing this yourself. Do it on every occasion, even if you know perfectly well the pistol is unloaded. By making this an instinctive habit you will avoid many risks of accidents; and you will show other people that you are a disciplined and trained pistol shot.

Always handle a pistol as a loaded weapon. Never carry it about in the hand among people, or wave it about, or keep clicking the trigger. The pistol should be kept in the holster on all occasions, and drawn only to do some definite exercise or to shoot. People frequently wave their pistols about; they get into exaggerated positions; and after each shot they fling their pistols up in the air and bring them back over their heads in a wild sweep, finishing up by turning and pointing the weapon at somebody behind, while excitedly making remarks about their last shot.

The correct way to fire at a target is this: —

Have a bench or narrow table in front of you with the ammunition laid on it. Walk up to the table, draw the pistol, prove it, load, take your correct grip, turn into your firing position, and hold the pistol pointing towards the target at full extent of the arm at 45 degrees to the ground.

Keeping the eyes on the target throughout, come up to the aim, fire, and lower the arm again to the position 45 degrees to the ground. Repeat this without hesitating or turning round, until you have fired all the cartridges. Then unload and replace the pistol immediately in the holster. Watch a disciplined shot at work. His pistol and arm move up and down from the 45 degrees position. He never turns round. He keeps his eyes on his target. His pistol always points to the front.

This holding at 45 degrees to the ground is an important habit to contract. Whenever you take a pistol in the hand hold it out at 45 degrees to the ground. Never point it at your foot or swing it past and behind you, which is so easy to do when shooting quickly. If you become lazy and let your pistol hang at your side, one day it will go off, and you will lose your foot. Hold it at 45 degrees; then, if it does go off, the bullet will go harmlessly into the ground.

———————

N. B. — When unloading an automatic pistol, after removing the magazine always pull the slide or breech back to eject the cartridge which remains in the chamber. If you forget to do this you will have an accident.

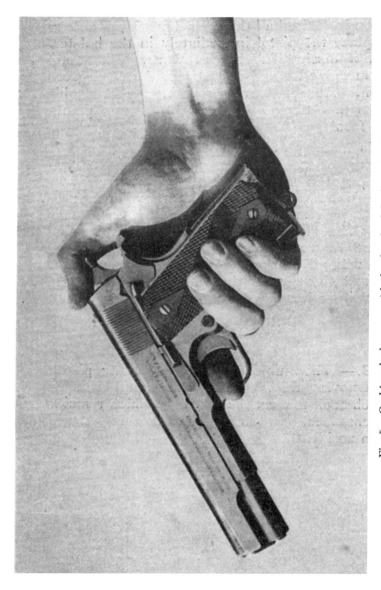

Fig. 5. — Cocking the hammer with the thumb of the firing hand.
(Note trigger finger is kept clear of the trigger whilst the thumb cocks the hammer.)

CHAPTER III

PISTOL SHOOTING EXERCISES.

Preliminary training in the pistol exercises is essential before firing. Constant practice at these exercises will render the manipulations of the pistol quick and instinctive. Exercises should be practised in conjunction with shooting on the range; and faults discovered while shooting should be rectified by renewed application to the exercises.

Rapid firing cannot, of course, be practised with an empty pistol. This needs ammunition.

For exercises dummy cartridges are needed, and a spare magazine.

There are two kinds of exercises:—
(1) Muscle exercises;
(2) Exercises for aiming and firing.

Muscle Exercises (for the ·45 Colt Automatic).

The object of these is to develop and render flexible the muscles needed in shooting but little used in ordinary life.

No. 1 Muscle Exercise.—Cocking the hammer by thumb.

Hold the pistol at 45 degrees to the ground with the hammer at half cock. Place the thumb on the hammer, and practise the quick cocking of the hammer by the upward fling of the pistol and arm.

Continue doing this until the cocking can be performed without any loss of time, and without any fumbling of the fingers. Then practise with the hammer not at half cock, but fully down; and also practise cocking whilst drawing from the holster.

It is most important to train the trigger finger to keep off the trigger whilst the thumb is cocking the hammer. Be very careful about this, and correct any tendency to hang on to the trigger by doing the special finger exercise, as in the illustration. This exercise reproduces the action of the fingers while firing the pistol.

No. 2 Muscle Exercise.—Muscle and Nerve Control.

Select an aiming mark three-quarters of an inch in diameter, twelve feet away, and hold the sights on to this mark for one minute.

This is an exercise for will power and nerve and muscle control only, and not a method of aiming and firing.

No. 3 Muscle Exercise.—Developing sense of direction and the power of quick alignment of sights.

Chalk a vertical line on the wall with a bull's-eye two inches above the end of the line. Stand about 12 feet away.

Hold the pistol at 45 degrees to the ground; and raise and lower the pistol up and down the vertical line, keeping the sights on the line. With practice the pistol should be able to be whipped up to the mark, and each time the sights should cut right through the bull's-eye.

It must be noted carefully whether the sights rise *together* to the mark. This will happen automatically if the grip is correct and the arm and wrist kept straight.

No. 4 Exercise.—Operating the safety lock by the thumb.

Cock the hammer and hold the pistol at full extent of the arm. Practise working the safety lock up and down by the thumb of the right hand.

No. 5 Muscle Exercise.—Quick Magazine Changing.

Pistol in ready position at hip, magazine empty, slide open.

Release the magazine by the thumb of the firing hand pressing on the magazine catch. Try to do this without altering the grip.

Insert a new magazine loaded with dummies, and let the slide down by operating the slide catch with the thumb of the firing hand.

Exercises for Aiming and Firing.
No. 6 Firing Exercise.—Snapshooting.

Load the magazine with dummies, or remove the magazine if no dummies are available. Hold the pistol in the right hand, pointing to the ground in front at 45 degrees, pistol turned over with back of hand uppermost.

Draw the slide back with the left hand, thereby cocking the action; and raise the pistol straight to the mark, squeezing off the trigger by a firm even pressure of the whole hand, just at the moment the sights touch the mark.

This trigger release requires careful practice. Trigger pressing is the whole thing in snapshooting.

The standard of rapidity is an accurate shot in two seconds.

No. 7 Firing Exercise.—Sense of direction shooting.

Proceed as for No. 6 Exercise, but fire by instinctive aim instead of aligning the sights. Immediately after firing look along the sights and quickly note where they are pointing, or work with another man aiming at his eye (prove pistol first).

No. 8 Firing Exercise.—Hip shooting.

Prove pistol. Practise rapidly aligning the pistol on to a man's body twelve feet away, holding the weapon at the hip whilst walking forward or coming round a corner. The instinctive "feel" of the hand must be learned to get this alignment automatic and accurate.

It will be found in all sense of direction exercises that great determination and force of will combined with fixing the eye firmly on the mark will help enormously in the instinctive alignment of the pistol.

Hip shooting is a method of high speed shooting. It must be practised mainly on the range, firing with ammunition.

No. 9 Firing Exercise.—Shooting from horseback.

Prove pistol. Whilst riding past various men holding the pistol pointing up, bring the pistol down as you pass to snap the shot off. The men will spot the accuracy of the throw.

Special Muscle Exercises for the Webley-Scott Pistol.
Rapid Cocking.

The pistol is difficult to cock with the thumb of the firing hand. The thumb of the disengaged hand must be used, and proficiency obtained in the quick manipulation of the hammer in this way.

Quick magazine changing.

With the Webley-Scott pistol the breech, when open, is released automatically by the insertion of a freshly loaded magazine. Therefore, in No. 5 exercise there is no necessity to release the breech stop with the thumb after inserting the loaded magazine (loaded with dummies).

No. 4 Exercise.

There is no independent safety catch with the pistol, therefore this exercise will not be needed.

The pistol may be carried about absolutely safe with the hammer cocked by withdrawing the trigger finger from the trigger guard and holding it along the side of the pistol.

General Note.

Exercises should be practised in the order given, methodically and regularly, muscle exercises always to commence with.

An exercise should be practised alternately with left and right hands for a number of times corresponding to the magazine capacity, seven, eight or ten shots, as the case may be.

This cultivates the useful habit of automatically counting the shots when firing.

A pause to rest must be made in between each exercise.

The Art of Shooting is the Touch on the Trigger.

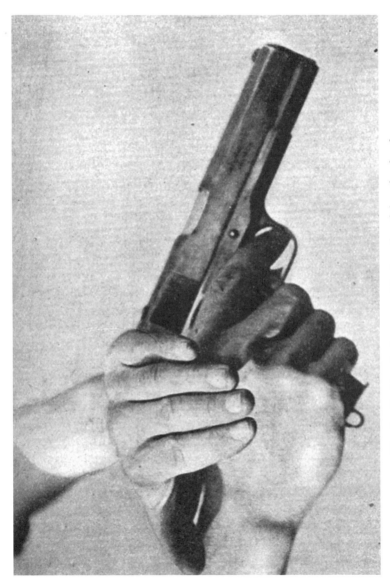

Fig. 6.—Cocking the hammer with the palm of the other hand.

CHAPTER IV.

THE THEORY OF SHOOTING WITH A
SINGLE-HANDED FIREARM.

As regards that vexed question of quick shooting as opposed to deliberate shooting, people who practise with firearms, generally strong-minded people, get very rigid views on the subject. Some condemn the deliberate aim, saying it should never be employed on any occasion, while others adhere to what they call the "quick deliberate aim."

It will be interesting to study and compare the different methods, and draw some definite conclusions from them.

Take, first, the quick deliberate aim method, in which the pistol is quickly aligned on the mark and the sights held for a moment while the trigger is released. The drawback to this method is that, when firing at a disappearing target, it is liable to encourage the worst of all faults—trigger snatching. The firer comes up and aligns his sights and holds on. Now, because the pistol is a single-handed weapon, used without support to the hand or arm, it is difficult to get dead steady; so the firer, however skilled or however steady his arm may be, never gets truly satisfied with his aim. This lack of satisfaction causes a delay in his trigger pressing. The longer he delays the more shaky he becomes. When at last he gets his aim "about right," he fears that he will wobble off the next moment, so he presses his trigger quickly, whereas he should press firmly and gradually. This quick pressure easily becomes a jerk, and so the shot goes wild.

For quick shooting against moving targets the author thinks it best to use the pistol according to its characteristics. It is a single-handed weapon — a weapon for movement, as opposed to a weapon for fixed aim, such as a two-handed weapon (rifle).

You should shoot with the single-handed weapon *while it is moving*. The pistol should be raised from below the mark usually; and the trigger pressing, the most vital thing in shooting, should be slow and continuous. It should commence when the arm starts to raise the pistol; and it should be so regulated as to release the trigger and throw the shot at the moment the sights reach the mark. Herein lies the difference to the quick deliberate aim method, in which the trigger pressing commences only *after* the sights have reached the mark.

The art of quick shooting lies in perfecting the automatic trigger squeeze, combining this with the upward lift of the pistol so that the bullet departs at the moment the sights intercept the line of sight from the eye to the target.

Suppose you are shooting at a disappearing target. As the target appears you raise the pistol and lead the sights to the mark by "sense of direction." The hand starts its squeeze of the trigger as the pistol is rising; and this squeeze is regulated with the speed of raising the arm in such a way that the trigger is. released automatically at the moment the sights reach the mark. The pistol continues its movement and does not for one instant "sit on the mark."

In shooting at a running target the same principle is applied—the sights are led to the mark by the arm; and the trigger is released at the moment the sights and the aiming mark meet. This gives the advantage of relatively slow trigger pressing, although shooting is quick because the whole time taken in raising the arm can be devoted to the trigger pressing. Trigger pressing is the most important thing in shooting.

The above explains the normal method of shooting; but it must be recognised that the method must depend somewhat on the two circumstances, the speed of shooting and the range. One would not shoot in the same way at 50 yards as one would at 5 yards.

The prevalent method of shooting with a revolver is single shot firing, cocking the hammer by thumb, and throwing the bullet by the upward fling of the arm, this method being used for all occasions and for all ranges. But the author has always upheld that the method of handling should vary according to the circumstance; and for close range work he advocates double action shooting from the hip, firing a stream of bullets, as opposed to single shot firing.

This principle is adaptable essentially to the automatic with its enormous rate of fire, large magazine capacity, and quick reloading. For close quarter work, say 5–30 feet, the pistol should be used from the hip. At medium ranges the pistol is fired by the upward throw of the arm, but without use of the sights. At long ranges the sights are used.

In concluding these few remarks on the theory of shooting, the author wishes to say that he does not lay down that any one theory is rigidly the only correct theory, and that all else is wrong. Pistol shooting is merely a matter of practice. Anybody can learn to shoot (that is, practical, useful shooting, not champion target or trick work); and he can adopt any method that comes easiest to him. But the author has explained the principles of shooting with the single-handed firearm, and has shown along what lines to work in order to become a "good and useful pistol shot."

The Trick Lies in the Trigger.

Fig. 7.—The .455 Webley-Scott (The British Naval Weapon).

CHAPTER V.

QUICK SHOOTING AT MOVING TARGETS.

Quick shooting, shooting at moving targets, and shooting while on the move yourself, requires a different system of training from deliberate shooting. You cannot claim to be a pistol shot unless you are a quick shot.

Quick shooting is certainly more interesting and far more practical. People like the spectacular effect of grouping their shots into the circumference of a coin, smashing bottles, etc. Close grouping should not be the test of shooting, but rather the rapidity with which a hit can be placed on the "man" target. Rapidity should be the first consideration, and grouping the second consideration.

Quick shooting depends upon sense of direction — the ability of the eye automatically to guide the hand to point and throw. Therefore, this principle should be applied, first, by selecting a definite aiming mark on the target, and, secondly, by concentrating one's whole attention on this definite mark.

Most people merely "cover" the target with the pistol; but it will be found every time that the selection of a definite aiming mark will always improve the accuracy of shooting. Again, the greater the concentration of the attention on the mark the closer the grouping will automatically become.

Snapshooting.

Two methods can be distinguished: —

1. When the target is exposed for sufficient time to take aim with the sights.

2. When the target is suddenly encountered at close range and there is no time to use the sights — shooting is done by sense of direction.

In shooting in self defence you have to decide simultaneously as the target appears how you are going to shoot — whether you are going to throw a shot dispensing with an alignment of the sights or whether you are going to use your sights. You will have to find out by practice on the range up to what distances you can rely to hit by shooting by sense of direction.

Snapshooting using the sights.

The method of firing is exactly as in No. 6 exercise.

If you are firing only single shots, using a pistol with an outside hammer with the chamber loaded, you will have to cock the hammer by thumb, like in using a revolver. If using a pistol with no outside hammer, the action must be kept at full cock with the safety bolt up. This safety bolt must be operated by the thumb of the firing hand, as the pistol is raised to the mark. If there is no cartridge ready in the chamber, the cartridge must be fed up from the magazine by "cocking by the slide," with the left hand.

The essential point is this — align the sights from below, and always bring the pistol up to the mark, as opposed to bringing it down from above.

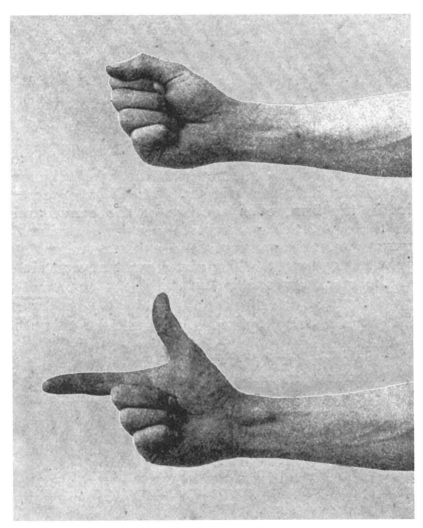

Fig. 8. — Finger exercise.
To train the trigger finger and the thumb to work
independently of the fingers gripping the butt.

You get greater speed and greater accuracy by coming up to the mark from below. Bringing the pistol down from above is to be used for shooting from horseback or from a motor bicycle. *Good trigger pressing is the whole secret of snapshooting.*

It is essential to adjust the trigger of your pistol to eliminate all "drag." Many automatics as made at present suffer from very badly adjusted triggers; and this quite upsets one's shooting.

Remember to squeeze with the whole hand, and never jerk the trigger. The whole secret lies in the firm, even squeeze of the hand, and the timing of this pressure to release the trigger just at the moment the sights intercept the line of sight to the target. The pistol must never "sit" on the mark for one instant.

Shooting by sense of direction.

This method is used for: —

1. Shooting at relatively close range (range depending upon the skill of the firer).
2. Shooting at great speed.
3. Shooting in the dark.

Here you dispense with your sights, and rely upon your correct grip and sense of direction to "throw the shot."

The harder the eye is fixed on the mark and the greater the concentration of the attention to a definite mark on the target, so the more accurate the shooting will be. Never cover the target roughly with the pistol, as many people do. Select one mark. If it is a man target, take the body or the chest. The head is a small mark, and a body wound is just as fatal generally as a hit in the head, owing to the great stopping power of the bullet, especially the big ·45 bullet.

It will be necessary to develop "sense of direction"—to develop and practise those muscles which control the quick raising and pointing of the pistol. No. 3 Exercise gives this accuracy.

When you can rely upon your sense of direction being right, you must practise the "timing of the trigger release," so that the bullet departs just at the moment the arm has raised the pistol to the correct alignment. You get this automatically with practice by the feel of the hand just as easily and automatically as you throw a stone to hit a mark in front of you.

An interesting experiment is to stand in front of a straight tree, 15 yards away, and throw stones underhand, trying to hit the tree trunk each time. This resembles pistol shooting in that the line of throw represents the "sense of direction"; the release of the stone from the hand represents the "trigger release."

You should practise on the range with a standing man target 5 yards in front, increasing the range later. Direct the eyes on to the mark, holding the pistol at 45 degrees to the ground. Throw the arm and pistol up to the target, squeezing off the trigger instinctively by the "feel of the hand.

The first thing to practise is "direction"; and the second thing is the "timing of the trigger release," or "elevation."

Rapid Firing.

The essential principle of rapid firing, perhaps the chief use of the automatic pistol, is slow aiming and rapid re-alignment of sights between shots. This does not mean slow shooting. By practising the art of quickly realigning the sights after firing for the next shot you will be able to save a tremendous amount of time; and this time you can devote to careful aiming and trigger pressing.

An untrained man will take hurried shots; his pistol will be shaking in the air; his hand will be jumping on the grip; and he will be slow to bring the sights back on to the mark between shots.

A trained man will do the opposite. His pistol will remain very steady; there will be little jump; and the time saved by this steadiness will be devoted to perfect aiming and trigger pressing.

A skilled revolver shot utilises the recoil of his revolver to help him in cocking the hammer and re-aligning the sights to the target; and he can shoot with great speed. But the automatic can score over the revolver in rapid firing by reason of the absorption of the recoil by the mechanism; and the pistol keeps nearer the mark the whole time while firing.

Practise holding the pistol in the hand, checking the upward jump; and try and bring the sights back to the mark instantly after firing, for the next shot. Keep the hand well high on the butt—as high as you can.

In re-aligning the sights to the mark it should be understood that they do not come back to the deliberate alignment, but to a point below the mark, and then

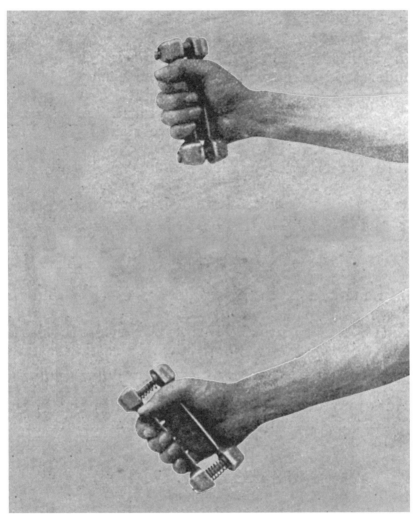

Fig. 9.— Dumb-bell exercise for grip and trigger squeeze.
To develop the shooting muscles and train the hand to
release the trigger by a squeeze of the whole hand.

lead up into the mark. Always shoot with the pistol on the move rising to the mark from below.

With practice you can learn the art of keeping the pistol moving and firing the whole time, and so gain tremendous speed. In rapid firing at several targets surrounding you, take them from right to left rather than from left to right.

Shooting at a crossing target.

As soon as the target appears the pistol should be raised to the mark, as for snapshooting. A slight swing of the body will bring the pistol to the mark, and the trigger is squeezed off at the moment the sights meet the aiming mark.

The advancing man.

The method is the same as for rapid firing. Shoot slowly and carefully at long range. It is often useful to use the pistol as a two-handed weapon at long range, lying down or resting the arm, keeping the eyes well away from the sights.

Targets advancing on the firer at close quarters may be engaged by hip shooting, sweeping the targets with a stream of bullets from right to left.

Hip Shooting.

This is the quickest method of firing, and the best method of handling the pistol in confined localities.

It is purely sense of direction work—fast "bullet squirting," for close range shooting.

Enlarged magazines, holding twenty rounds, are needed.

By constant practice the instinctive alignment of the pistol can be sensed by the feel of the hand.

Shooting on the move, or from horseback.

The usual way is to hold the pistol pointing up and to bring it down on the target, instead of bringing it up from beneath, as in snapshooting and rapid firing from a stationary position.

Shooting from horseback is difficult, and needs practice, particularly if the target itself is moving. Still, it is a most useful and practical method of shooting, and should be learnt.

When running on the ground, shooting can be done from the hip; and if you shoot in this way, instead of halting to shoot from a stationary position, you will find it a good way to disconcert your opponents when they outnumber you.

———————

NOTE.—Shoot from the hip at close quarters. "Throw your shot" at medium ranges, with a full arm throw. Shoot with your sights at long ranges.

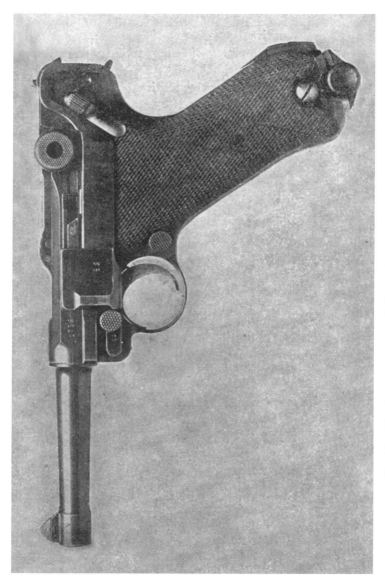

Fig. 10.— The 9 mm. Lugar Parabellum (the German military automatic).

CHAPTER VI.

HOW TO PRACTISE ON THE RANGE.

Before starting to shoot it is necessary to have practised the exercises. Most people's idea of pistol shooting is to blaze off ammunition on the range, until their arm becomes too tired to continue. They practise the wrong kind of shooting, and contract faults which are difficult to overcome later.

Proficiency is gained by careful training in the exercises, combined with firing on the range. Range practices should be considered as the application of the exercises. On the range mistakes and faults will be revealed, and these must be corrected by renewed application to those exercises which will remedy the particular faults.

System is the secret of training. Exercises should be done regularly and at regular times of the day. Shooting should be practised at regular hours each day. There is an old saying that a watch works best if wound up at regular times. This also is the same in pistol shooting, or, for that matter, in any form of human physical training.

If you have never fired with a pistol before, the first thing to do will be to accustom yourself to the shock of discharge. Stand on the range about ten yards from the stop butts; load, and, holding the pistol at the hip, fire shots off slowly. This exercise is best practised with the pistol at the hip, because there is less likelihood of getting bitten at the commencement of one's training with the flinching habit.

Flinching and trigger snatching are the two great evils.

Flinching can be overcome by the above exercise of slow firing from the hip and concentrating the determination and force of will not to allow oneself to be affected in the smallest way by the explosion of the cartridge. Reason will tell you that nothing can harm you; nothing can hit you in the face; nothing can strain your wrist and arm.

A good flinching test can be carried out by firing with the magazine loaded with live rounds interspersed with dummies. Errors in flinching will be revealed by the jerk or dip of the pistol when the dummy round is struck.

Force of will and constant firing will overcome flinching. The trigger pressing must be automatic and almost subconscious. There must be no anticipation of the shock of discharge, and no shutting of the eyes.

The next step will be to practise trigger pressing. Trigger pressing is the basis of pistol shooting; and it is no use to start snapshooting until proficiency is attained in the following trigger pressing tests

First Trigger Pressing Exercise and Test.

Correct squeezing.

Put up a trigger pressing target, 4ft. by 4ft., with a centre black line down the middle of the target about 2ft. long. Range, 10 yards. Load and get ready. Raise the pistol by a steady lift of the arm. As the pistol travels up the line, gradually tighten the squeeze of the whole hand, and, *while the pistol is moving,* squeeze off the trigger. Watch the sights as they travel up the line. It will not matter at what moment you release the trigger at the commencement, middle or end of the line.

Now, if you press correctly, each shot will be thrown on the black line. If you press incorrectly or jerk the trigger the shots will be thrown off the line.

Second Trigger Pressing Exercise.

The timing of the trigger release.

After proficiency in correct trigger squeezing is gained by the preceding exercise, the next thing to do will be the "timing of the trigger release."

Fig. 11. — Mauser Automatic.

Range, 10 yards. Action cocked. This time fix the eyes on the top end of the line on the target. Raise the pistol straight up the line, tightening the pressure of the hand as the pistol nears the mark, and so regulate this pressure that the trigger is timed to fire just at the moment the sights reach the end of the line.

With practice you will soon be able to get this knack of the timing of the trigger release; and you will be able to throw your shots into a four inch group at the top of the line.

Go on practising this exercise, and at the same time increase your speed of raising the arm.

Faults and their correction.

1. A scattered group all over the target—inability to come steadily up the line.

> *Cause*—A shaky arm.
>
> *Remedy*—Devote attention to No. 2 and
>   No. 3 muscle exercises.

2. A scattered group low left on the target (with right hand).

> *Cause*—Trigger snatching.
>
> *Remedy*—Practise trigger pressing, dumbbell
>   exercises for grip and trigger squeeze.
>
>   Trigger snatching is the very worst of all faults; and, unless it is conquered, no useful shooting can be done.

3. A shot group left or right, but level with the aiming mark.

Cause—Trigger pressing is correct as regards the uniform squeeze, but the pressure is being exerted out of the line of the axis of the barrel.

Remedy—Look to the position of the finger on the trigger (test the accuracy of the sighting of the pistol by getting another man to shoot with it).

4. A small group, but high or low on the target.

   Cause—Releasing trigger a little too late or a little too soon. Incorrect use of sights, or possibly the sights of the pistol need adjustment.

Snapshooting.

After passing the two trigger pressing exercises and tests you will be ready to commence snapshooting.

Range, 10 yards. Practise at a disappearing target with three seconds exposure for each shot.

Do not try to take a deliberate aim or "quick deliberate aim." Raise the pistol straight to the mark and release the trigger as the sights touch the mark, without hesitation or delay.

If firing at a man figure target, paste on a white spot, to represent the aiming mark.

STANDARD TESTS.

Snapshooting, 3 seconds exposure, 10 yards, 4in. group, 7 shots.

Snapshooting, 3 seconds exposure, 15 yards, 6in. group, 7 shots.

Snapshooting, 3 seconds exposure, 20 yards, 8in. group, 7 shots.

After passing these tests, go on to snapshooting at two seconds exposure at all ranges, 10—20 yards.

Rapid Firing.

After passing the snapshooting tests, commence rapid firing. Range, 10 yards, 7 shots in 15 seconds. Remember the essential principle of rapid firing—quick alignment of the sights, saving time for careful aiming and trigger pressing. This is the secret of rapid firing.

Go slow at first; and don't race. Speed will come with practice.

Work up to a standard of 7 hits on a man target in 10 seconds, at 20 yards.

Advanced Shooting.

A course of advanced shooting should include the following practices (the standard given is for an average good shot).

1. Snapshooting by sense of direction.

(Instinctive aiming without using the sights.)
Practise hitting a man target at 5 yards one second for each shot. Increase the range to 15 yards; work up to half a second a shot.

2. Rapid Firing.

Work up to a standard of one hit per second at 20 yards, full length man target.

3. Long range advanced snapshooting.

A special snapshooting range, as described in the notes on range construction, will be needed. The targets are hidden, and appear each at a different place and at a different range. Any ranges up to 150 yards. The targets are exposed for varying lengths of time, unknown to the firer. Targets can be exposed singly and then two or three at a time.

4. The crossing or running target.

Range, 20 yards, with the target moving at the pace of a walk and then at a run. Practise shooting at 50 yards at a large target cut to the shape of a man riding a horse, worked mechanically on a trolley and rails.

5. Advancing targets.

6. Hip shooting.

Ranges, 5—10 yards. Standard, 7 hits in 4 seconds. Full length man target. Half a second a shot is the standard of hip shooting.

7. Shooting on the move.

Put up 7 targets, all in different positions, from 10—40 yards. Advance at the run over a distance of 20 yards and throw a shot on to each target whilst running.

Standard, 7 hits in 15 seconds, including time taken to advance.

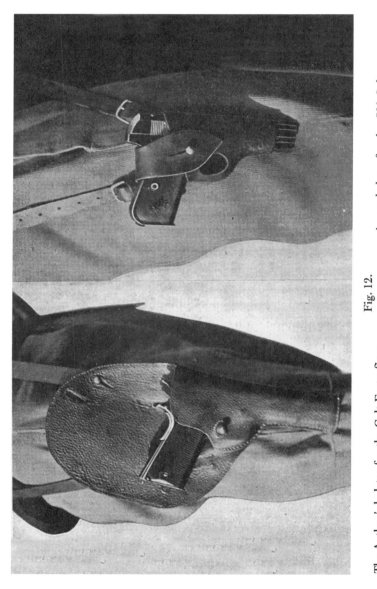

The Author's holster for the Colt Forty-fiver.   Fig. 12.   A neat holster for the ·380 Colt.

NOTE.—The flap can be buttoned up (as shown) or down.

Chapter VII.

PISTOL SHOOTING IN SELF DEFENCE.

In self defence the first essential is confidence in your weapon. Many people lack confidence in the pistol; and, of course, when that is the case they naturally would put up a very poor show in an actual fight. Now, the way to gain confidence in your weapon is this: You must first of all learn to use it; and then you must find out just what you can do with it.

By the pistol exercises you can learn to handle the pistol; and by shooting at each of the different kinds of moving targets on the range you will find out what chances you will have of hitting "man" targets in real life.

All the characteristics emphasize the utility of a pistol for self defence; and a study of the characteristics should be sufficient to convert anybody who may lack confidence in the weapon. The characteristics show that the weapon, by its short barrel and portability, is the best weapon for shooting at targets of opportunity—targets that suddenly appear and disappear; targets that advance towards the firer; and targets that appear in all directions, surrounding the firer.

The pistol is portable, handy and easy to conceal. It is suited for confined localities. It can be used equally well in either hand; and you can shoot with two pistols at once. Lastly, the stopping power is tremendous, owing to the big bullet; and you need hit a man only once in any part of his body to stop him, although he may be rushing you.

The first essential was confidence. Now the second essential is rapidity. Remember that the pistol is fundamentally a weapon for quick shooting, so, in order to profit by its characteristics and advantages, you must train for speed shooting above everything. Work at the elementary exercises for trigger pressing and snap-shooting, and also that important muscle exercise for pointing and automatically aligning the sights by the quick raising of the arm.

The two essentials—confidence and rapidity—are necessary also to each other. You cannot do with one and not the other. A man who lacks confidence would do best to shoot very slowly, as he will certainly be erratic and wild if he tries to shoot too quickly.

In self defence your targets are nearly always at close range; and you should engage those close range targets by sense of direction shooting, firing either from the hip or throwing the shot by the upward fling of the extended arm. You must find out by practice up to what range you can rely upon yourself to hit when shooting by instinctive aim, dispensing with the sights, so when the moment comes you will be able to decide at once how you are going to shoot—whether you are going to "throw your shot" or whether you are going to use your sights.

When your adversary is dangerous, shooting simultaneously at you, the best thing to do is this: Throw a shot as fast as ever you can; shoot like lightning. Your bullet will whizz past him and the moral effect will be tremendous, even if the bullet does not hit him. It will completely upset his aim, and delay him a second or two. This delay will give you the drop on him; and you will have a great chance for your second shot, steady and accurate right at his heart. If his first shot goes off before you shoot again you will find the bullet will go wild invariably.

By carrying your weapon at your hip you will be ready to get into action the moment you see your target. You fire from the hip as you are lifting the arm and pistol to the normal firing position to take aim; and with practice you can fire these two shots just as quickly as an ordinary man takes to fire one shot.

Moral forces are of great importance. Play upon the moral factor. When you meet an enemy, don't fire one single slow shot, but let out a whole stream of metal at him.

To supplement your skill in shooting there are some further points to remember, all of which help in "getting into action quickly."

Carry your pistol when out of the holster in the hip shooting position. Here it is safe, not pointing at your foot, and ready for the first shot.

Generally, however, it is best to keep the pistol in the holster, and provide yourself with such a holster that you can draw and shoot very quickly from it. The holster should hang low on the leg, at a height that the hand reaches the butt comfortably and easily. If it is carried very low it may be secured from dangling by using a supplementary cord or strap round the leg.

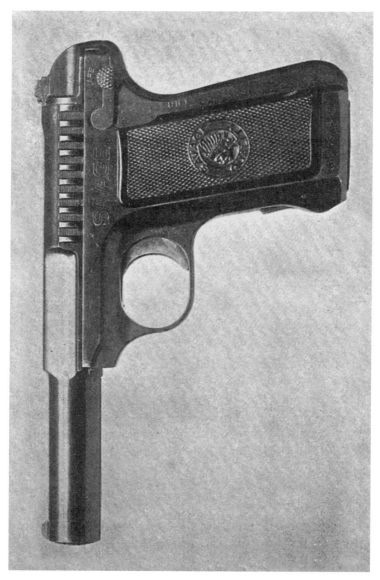

Fig. 13.—The .380 Savage. An excellent small automatic for self defense.

The pistol holster, as illustrated, is most comfortable to wear. It can be carried in any position at the side or behind the back. The pistol is held tight, and never falls out, even when riding and jumping; but still it draws quickly, because the hand goes straight to the butt, and there is no flap to undo. In the normal position a stud on the strap holds the flap up. The flap can, however, be folded down to protect the pistol against rain, etc.

You should practise drawing and shooting from the holster. Stand in front of a man-sized target at 15 yards. Try and draw the pistol, and throw a shot on in one second. Cock the hammer for the first shot as you draw, or else keep the action cocked and operate the safety lock with the thumb.

When shooting at a man's body always select a definite aiming mark on the body or chest (in preference to the head), and rivet the eyes and whole attention to this definite mark. The power of the eye to control the pointing of the hand is the basis of shooting with the single-handed firearm; and it will be found in every case that the closer the concentration of the mind (through the eye) so the closer will be the grouping of the shots.

If you have several enemies around you, it is best to take them from right to left (with the right hand). It is easier to bring the pistol across this way than from left to right. But, of course, if the left hand man were the most dangerous, you would have to take him first, despite this rule.

If outnumbered or hard pressed, it is best to keep moving while you shoot, instead of maintaining a fixed position.

In the dark you must not attempt to aim with the sights, but rather shoot by sense of direction. Let your eye guide your hand. Generally you can see your enemy as a shape or shadow. Practise shooting at sounds in the dark. Crouch low on the ground, because nearly everybody shoots high in the dark, and so you will escape the other man's bullet, and also at the same time conceal yourself.

Fire three rounds rapid from the hip. Jump away to another position and fire again. This will confuse and demoralise your man, even if one of your shots do not hit him.

Handling the pistol in houses, round corners, and in confined localities.

An important point to remember in working with a pistol inside houses, along passages, at street corners, in woods and behind bushes is about changing the pistol from one hand to the other when coming round a corner. You will then be able to get into action quicker, and also expose the least part of your body.

Shooting from the hip is the best way to use the weapon at close quarters, because the shot can be fired without delay the moment the target is met. The barrel comes straight on to the target when coming round a corner.

Never be caught with an empty pistol. Eject the empty or nearly empty magazine without altering the grip of the firing hand. This can be done easily with most automatics. Feed the new loaded magazine in with the other hand.

An enlarged magazine, such as that to be obtained for the ·45 Colt, to hold twenty rounds, is most useful.

Handling an empty pistol.

Do not change the pistol over and hold it by the barrel, because this tells the tale that it is unloaded, and also invites the other man to seize the grip. If he does this he can easily wrench the pistol from your grasp.

Retaining the correct grip yourself, lunge for your opponent's neck or face with the full weight of your body behind the thrust. Deal a swinging blow across the face. If on a higher level than the other man, bring the pistol down like a hammer on top of his head, hitting him with the butt.

To take a man's pistol or revolver out of his hand, seize it by the barrel and give a very sharp and sudden jerk upwards and towards his body.

The question of what pistol to use for self defence is discussed in the next chapter.

Last Word.

1. Pistols and revolvers are the quickest and handiest firearms in the world.

2. Anybody can learn pistol shooting. It is merely a matter of practice.

3. If you are a good pistol shot, you will have nothing to fear from any man in the world.

CHAPTER VIII.

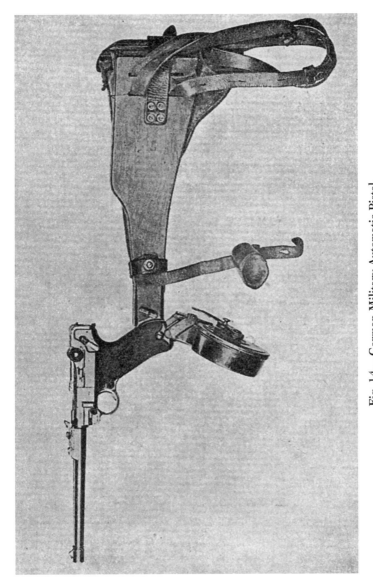

Fig. 14.—German Military Automatic Pistol.
The long-barrelled Parabellum attached to stock holster for use as a two-handed weapon.
Tangent backsight and large capacity magazine.

TYPES OF AUTOMATIC PISTOLS.

A considerable controversy exists between the rival merits of the revolver and automatic pistol. The revolver is the older weapon, and the weapon still used by the larger number of people who carry firearms for self defence. Having the advantage of being first in the field, it still solidly maintains its favour. Again, the revolver, being the older weapon, has reached high degree of perfection in design and construction.

The automatic pistol, however, is the weapon of the future.

Many people condemn the pistol, comparing with the revolver, but they forget that the automatic is only in its youth, and the defects that cling to it at present are not necessary defects. They are defects only of design; and they can be, and will be, remedied in the future.

War gives impetus to the evolution of firearms; and the experiences of the Great European Conflict point distinctly to the development of the short-barrelled, portable, automatic firearm with large magazine capacity. This tendency may express itself in the appearance of a two-handed weapon, such as an automatic rifle or a single-handed automatic weapon. It is unlikely that the single-handed weapon will displace the two-handed one; but the value and scope of the former will come to be more fully appreciated in the future; and it will be more extensively employed than at present.

Let us tabulate the characteristics, advantages and disadvantages of the automatic pistol.

Fig. 15

Diagram showing the disadvantage for quick shooting by instinctive aim of a square-handled pistol compared to one with a sloping handle.

Comes straight on.

Points low; wrist has to be bent up

ADVANTAGES.

1. Tremendous rapidity of firing.
2. Simplicity of firing—one hand alone needed and relatively little action needed in the fingers beyond trigger pressing.
3. Large magazine capacity. The modern automatic can be used with enlarged magazines, to hold twenty rounds or more.
4. Rapidity of reloading. A most important point as regards a firearm intended for close-quarter work.
5. Portability. Being flat, is easily carried or concealed.
6. Little shock of discharge or recoil. An advantage in rapid firing.

DISADVANTAGES.

1. Many automatics have butts at right angles to the barrel, which prevents the instinctive alignment of the sights by the fact of pointing (the basis of correct grip). The pistol cannot be fired by instinctive aim, and, therefore, fails in the primary use of the single-handed firearm. But this defect is only one of design. It can be easily remedied by fitting a properly shaped butt.
2. Liable to jamb with dirt or by use of a different make of ammunition.
3. Misfire causes a relatively long delay, and needs two hands to rectify.

4. Rather a dangerous weapon in the hands of a care-less or inexperienced man, because the action of unloading is a double action. Not only must the magazine be removed, but the remaining round in the chamber must also be removed, which careless people forget.
5. Less stopping power than the lead bullet used in the revolver.

POINTS ABOUT THE AUTOMATIC PISTOL.

Let us now see what points should be looked for when choosing a weapon. Some of the points enumerated below do not exist at present in any of the pistols made, but they are suggested as being needed to make the automatic a perfect weapon.

1. General design.

The pistol must be of simple mechanism and easily stripped by hand alone. The area of the frictional surface must be as small as possible.

2. The Butt.

The butt should be at a considerable slant, in order to bring the sights into the line of sight by taking a natural and comfortable grip. The butt should be of ample length, projecting below the little finger, even for a man with a big hand. The straight grips fitting to automatics are much inferior to the curved grips of revolvers. Although the magazine, fitting inside the butt, is straight and oblong, there is no reason why the butt should have the same shape outside as the magazine inside. The advantage of the curved, rounded stock of the revolver is that the hand can grip in any position, either high or low—the higher the grip the higher the foresight is raised.

With a revolver one can adjust the hand to give a perfect automatic alignment of the sights—

in fact, get a proper grip. With the straight stocks of automatics there is little choice in the adjustment of the hand.

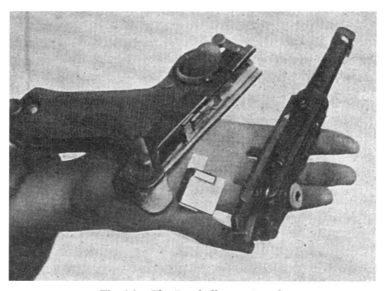

Fig. 16.—The Parabellum stripped.
Showing simplicity of construction—an important feature in the design of an automatic.

3. The Barrel.

The design of the mechanism must always be such that the barrel is made to recoil with the recoiling portions, and not be fixed.

If the barrel is fixed the extraction of the cartridge will commence the moment the cartridge is fired, and before the bullet has left the muzzle. Therefore, there will result a serious loss of gas behind the bullet; and fouling will clog the mechanism. In modern pistols the barrel recoils for a short distance with the recoiling portions before the extraction of the cartridge commences.

The bore should be ·45 to get good stopping power.

When the automatic first appeared people asserted that it could not be made for bigger bores than ·38; but now many models are made for ·45 bore, and this obstructionist assertion has fallen to the ground. In the same way the present objections and defects in the automatic will also be overcome, despite the head shakings of stick-in-the-mud people.

When Stephenson drove his first steam engine people shot at him from behind a hedge. But it is fortunate that those people had not done their pistol exercises, for they failed even to hit the steam engine.

The length of the barrel should certainly be longer than the usual custom at present. The long barrel has considerable advantages; and, if made of good steel, it may be thin and light, when there will be little loss in "balance." A free barrel, such as that of the ·22 Colt and the Parabellum, is preferable to a barrel encased in the slide. A better balance is obtained.

4. Balance.

Balance depends upon two things: —
   (i.) Getting the weight well into the palm of the hand;
   (ii.) Getting the hand high on the butt near the axis of the barrel.

Some pistols have magazines in front of the trigger, which spoils the balance. A long barrel (within limits, provided it is thin and light) improves the balance; certainly it improves the accuracy of shooting.

5. The Magazine.

The best position for the magazine is in the stock. All pistols should be adaptable to take enlarged magazines, holding twenty rounds.

The magazine removal must be automatic, and be operated by the thumb of the firing hand without altering the grip.

Some simple device, such as an inspection window in the side of the stock, coinciding with a slot in the magazine, should be provided, so that one can tell at a glance how many rounds have been fired and how many remain.

There should be a thumb-piece, as in the Parabellum magazine, for depressing the magazine platform by hand, which assists in the quick and easy loading of the magazine.

Some pistols are loaded by a clip of cartridges pressed down into the magazine from above; but this is not such a good method as changing the magazine itself for a fresh loaded one.

6. The Hammer.

It is an advantage to have an outside hammer, because then the pistol can be kept ready for action with a round in the chamber. For firing the first shot the hammer may be cocked by the thumb, as the pistol is drawn from the holster.

If there is no outside hammer the striker spring must be kept compressed, and the safety lock applied. This will be bad for the spring, and also will be dangerous.

The hammer should be capable of being placed, as in the Colt, at half cock or full cock. It should be broad and spoon-like, and comfortable and easy to work with the thumb.

7. The Trigger.

The art of trigger pressing is nine-tenths of pistol shooting, therefore the trigger mechanism must be perfect. The trigger should slide through without the slightest drag.

The revolver scores over the automatic in its exquisitely sweet trigger release. Revolvers, have rotating hammers and triggers; and one *rolls* off the other. In the automatic there is less room, owing to the magazine. The trigger mechanism is rather crude; and the trigger jerks and drags.

The trigger mechanism of all automatics needs improvement.

The trigger itself should be close into the hand. The farther the forefinger has to stretch the more the liability to snatch instead of squeeze. The trigger should be broad and comfortable to press.

The pull should not exceed 5lb., and can be usefully 2lb. to 3lb.

8. Sights.

The present sights of automatics are bad. The best target shooting sights are the "Colt Partridge" and the "Walter Winans." The best quick shooting sight for firing at a dark target or a man's body is an open U backsight, with horizontal shoulders, and a white metal bead foresight. The tip of the foresight is inclined off at 45 degrees to the line of sight; and this inclined surface catches the light and causes the foresight to shine up as a sparkling white spot. This sight is extremely quickly aligned on a dark target.

The backsight should be adjustable laterally, and the foresight vertically.

9. Automatic Slide, or Breech Stop.

This important fitting provides for the slide to remain open after the last shot is fired. This prevents one being caught with an empty pistol.

When the slide, or breech, is open the insertion of a new loaded magazine should automatically release the slide stop, thereby letting the slide fly forward and automatically feed the first cartridge from the magazine into the chamber.

10. Safety Lock.

This should be capable of operation by the thumb of the firing hand from *either* side of the pistol.

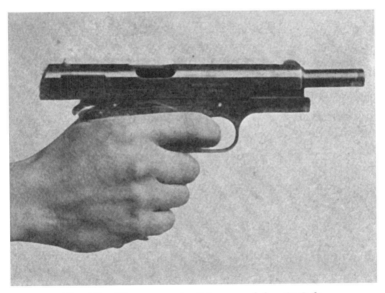

Fig. 17.—The automatic slide stop of the ·45 Colt.
Note.—Slide remains open after last cartridge is fired.

A safety lock provided only on the left side prevents the pistol being used in the left hand unless the use of the lock is dispensed with.

The lock should be at "safety" when in the up position, and at "fire" when down. This is a defect in the Parabellum, making it awkward to operate; and it enables an enemy to put the pistol out of action by pressing the lock down.

11. The Maxim Attachment.

An attachment should be fitted to the pistol to be worked by the thumb of the firing hand, to allow the pistol to fire single shots, or, by operating the special attachment, to maxim by continuous fire.

This subsidiary attachment, used with an enlarged magazine, would be of enormous use for self defence, when surrounded by enemies at close quarters—twenty men could be cut down by one sweep of the hand.

The author considers this feature will be one of the principal improvements in the automatic of the future, although in saying it he fully expects to be made a target for criticism and abuse by a certain section of people.

Fig. 18.—The 9 mm. Steyr Austrian Automatic (clip loading).

DIFFERENT TYPES OF PISTOLS.

The ·45 Colt Automatic (U.S. Government) Model.

Length of barrel	. . . . . .	5 inches.
Total length . . .	. . . . . .	8 1/2 inches.
Weight . . .	. . . . . .	39 ounces.
Magazines . . .	. . .	7 shots and 20 shots.

This excellent automatic embodies many of the needed improvements which have been already enumerated and discussed. A sloping butt is provided. The slide remains open after the last shot has been fired. The slide catch, magazine release and safety lock can all be operated by the thumb of the firing hand.

The outside hammer can be placed at full or half cock; and it can be operated by the thumb on drawing the pistol from the holster. (The hammer could be improved, however, by making it broader and more spoon shaped.)

The automatic grip safety prevents the pistol from being discharged unless the hand takes a proper grip of the butt.

The foresight is fixed, but the backsight is adjustable laterally.

The ·38 Colt Military Model.

Length of barrel	. . . . . .	6 inches.
Total length . . .	. . . . . .	9 inches.
Weight . . .	. . . . . .	38 ounces.
Magazines . . .	. . . . . .	8 shots.

This is a good pistol, having the advantage of a long barrel, but the disadvantage of a square grip. The slide remains open after the last cartridge is fired; and the slide stop is operated by the thumb of the firing hand.

The ·380 and ·320 Pocket Models
Colt Hammerless Pistols.

Length of barrel	. . . . . .	3 3/4 inches.
Total length . . .	. . . . . .	6 3/4 inches.
Weight . . .	. . . . . .	23 ounces.
Magazines . . .	.380, 7 shots; .320, 8 shots.	

These pistols are handy and portable, and very suitable for carrying in the pocket.

There are two safety devices; and these indicate also when the pistol is cocked. One is the slide lock, which can be operated by the thumb to engage in the slide cut when the action is cocked, and so lock the trigger. The other is the automatic grip safety.

Fig. 19.—The ·22 Colt Target Model Automatic

The ·22 Target Model Colt.

Length of barrel	. . . . . .	6 1/2 inches.
Total length . . .	. . . . . .	10 1/2 inches.
Weight . . .	. . . . . .	28 ounces.
Magazine . . .	. . . . . .	10 shots.
Sights . . .	Bead foresight, adjustable for elevation; rear sight adjustable for direction.	
Distance between sights	. . .	9 inches.

This is in every way a most excellent pistol. It takes the ·22 long rifle greased cartridges, which are cheap and always easily obtained. Great accuracy of shooting is obtained, on account of the accurate ·22 ammunition used, the long barrel and long distance between the sights and the sights being adjustable. Again, a little pistol of this kind enables one to practise shooting at any time, without the necessity of a range for safety. There is little noise of firing; and the bullet has good stopping power for small game shooting.

The grip is particularly comfortable and well shaped. A safety lock is provided on the left side of the pistol; to be operated by the thumb in every respect this is a most excellent and well designed small-bore automatic.

The ·380 and ·320 Savage Pistols.

The ·380 calibre has a 9 shot magazine, barrel 4 1/4 inches, weight 21ozs., total length 7 inches.

The ·320 calibre has a 10 shot magazine, barrel 3 3/4 inches, weight 19ozs., and, total length 6 1/2 inches.

The Savage are excellent pocket pistols of clever design and simple mechanism. They can be stripped by hand alone in a few seconds; and there are no small parts to lose.

To strip.
Draw the slide back and lock it by raising the safety catch. Give the bolt a half turn and remove it. Let the safety catch down; and the barrel and recoil spring will slide forward off the body.

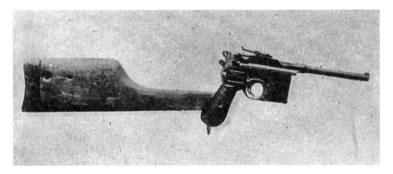

Fig. 20a.—A Mauser attached to holster stock.

The Webley-Scott High Velocity Automatic Pistol.

This automatic is made in ·455 and ·38 calibre.
The distinctive feature of the pistol is the simplicity of its construction, simplicity of stripping, and general reliability for shooting.

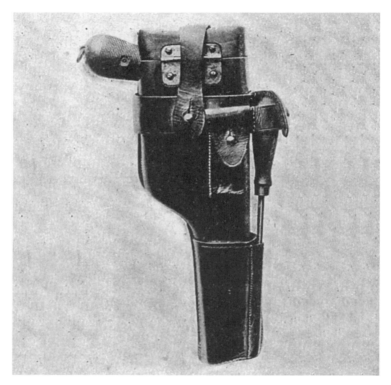

Fig. 20b.—The Mauser in holster.

Other features of the pistol are:—

1. Action remains open after last shot is fired.
2. Outside hammer.
3. Automatic safety lock.
4. Adjustable sights.
5. Length, 8 1/2 inches and 8 inches.
6. Weight, 36ozs. and 33ozs.

The 9mm. Lugar Parabellum Automatic Pistol.

The design is most efficient, and the mechanism is simple; and, generally speaking, the pistol goes a long way to fulfilling the essential requirements of the perfect automatic.

The features of the pistol are: —

1. The excellent long, sloping butt. A natural grip of the hand brings the sights absolutely straight on the mark.
2. Extremely easy to strip and assemble.
3. Action remains open after the last cartridge is fired.
4. Excellent trigger.
5. Little liability to stoppage or jamb through dirt.
6. Good sights (adjustable foresight).
7. Barrel recoils with recoiling portions.

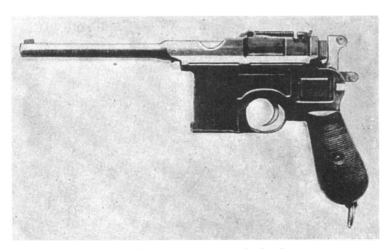

Fig. 20c. — The 9 mm. Mauser (clip loading).

8. Cocking action easy and quick to work.
9. No outside hammer—a disadvantage.
10. Safety catch on left side of pistol. At "safe" when down and "fire" when up. (N.B.—The reverse would be better and more convenient.)
11. Very short barrel; but good distance between the sights.
12. Magazine quickly removable without altering the grip. Magazine is quick to reload, owing to the provision of a thumb piece to depress the magazine platform.

To strip the pistol.
1. Remove the magazine.
2. Pull back recoiling portions and hold back.
3. Depress the catch in front of the trigger, and remove the side plate behind this catch.
4. Let recoiling portions go forward again, when they will slide off the body.

The Trigger!

The Trigger!!

The Trigger!!!

COMPONENT PARTS COLT AUTOMATIC PISTOL
(Caliber .45, Government Model.)

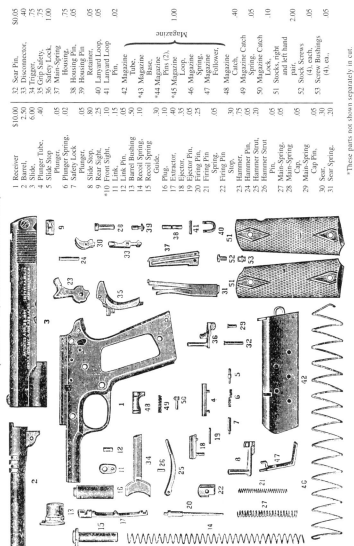

1	Receiver	$10.00
2	Barrel,	2.50
3	Slide,	6.00
4	Plunger Tube,	.40
5	Slide Stop Plunger,	.05
6	Plunger Spring,	.02
7	Safety Lock Plunger,	.05
8	Slide Stop,	.80
9	Rear Sight,	.25
*10	Front Sight,	.10
11	Link,	.15
12	Link Pin,	.05
13	Barrel Bushing	.50
14	Recoil Spring,	.10
15	Recoil Spring Guide,	.30
16	Plug,	.10
17	Extractor,	.40
18	Ejector,	.35
19	Ejector Pin,	.05
20	Firing Pin,	.25
21	Firing Pin Spring,	.05
22	Firing Pin Stop,	.30
23	Hammer,	.75
24	Hammer Pin,	.05
25	Hammer Strut,	.20
26	Hammer Strut Pin,	.05
27	Main-Spring,	.05
28	Main-Spring Cap,	.05
29	Main-Spring Cap Pin,	.05
30	Sear,	.30
31	Sear Spring,	.20
32	Sear Pin,	$0.05
33	Disconnector,	.40
34	Trigger,	.75
35	Grip Safety,	.75
36	Safety Lock,	1.00
37	Main-Spring Housing,	.75
38	Housing Pin,	.05
39	Housing Pin Retainer,	.05
40	Lanyard Loop,	.05
41	Lanyard Loop Pin,	.02
42	Magazine Tube,	1.00
*43	Magazine Base,	
**44	Magazine Pins (2),	
*45	Magazine Loop,	
46	Magazine Spring,	
47	Magazine Follower,	
48	Magazine Catch,	.40
49	Magazine Catch Spring,	.05
50	Magazine Catch Lock,	.10
51	Stocks, right and left hand pair,	2.00
52	Stock Screws (4), each,	.05
53	Screw Bushings (4), ea.,	.05

(Parts 42–47 bracketed as "Magazine")

*These parts not shown separately in cut.

Fig. 21.

CHAPTER IX

THE MECHANISM OF THE ·45 COLT AUTOMATIC.

How to strip the pistol.

Stripping the Slide from the Receiver (body).

1. Remove magazine by pressing the magazine catch behind trigger on left side of pistol.
2. Push in the plug below the barrel at the muzzle.
3. Give the barrel bushing a quarter turn to the right and remove the plug, recoil spring, and barrel bushing.
4. Draw the slide back and push the slide stop up to engage in the second (smaller) recess cut in the side of the slide.
5. The slide stop will now lift out.
6. Remove the slide, barrel, recoil spring guide.

To re-assemble.

1. Replace barrel inside the slide, and also the recoil spring guide, with the flanged end next to the link on under side of barrel.
2. Replace slide from muzzle end on to receiver (body).
3. Replace slide stop so that the pin goes through the link on the under side of the barrel. Pull the slide back till the slide stop is opposite the smaller recess in the slide; and then push the slide stop home.

4. Push slide right forward and replace barrel bushing.
5. Replace recoil spring and plug.
6. Push plug home, compressing the recoil spring; and turn the barrel bushing into place on top of plug.
7. Replace magazine.

To strip the hammer and trigger mechanism.
1. Push out mainspring housing pin at end of butt.
2. Pull out mainspring housing.
3. Remove sear spring.
4. Remove safety lock. First draw hammer back. With right hand press in safety lock pivot on right side of pistol; and with left hand work safety lock up and down until it clicks out.
5. Remove grip safety.
6. Press out hammer pin from right side of pistol; and remove hammer with its strut pin.
7. Remove sear pin, sear and disconnector.
8. Remove magazine catch lock, magazine catch and spring.
9. Slide out trigger from back of pistol.

To re-assemble—Hold pistol in left hand, muzzle to ground.
1. Replace trigger.
2. Replace magazine catch, spring and catch lock.
3. Replace disconnector.
4. Replace sear and sear pin (inserting from left side).
5. Replace hammer and its axis pin (from left side).
6. Replace sear spring.

7. Replace mainspring housing, but not completely, sufficient to hold sear spring in place.
8. Replace grip safety.
9. Draw hammer back and replace safety lock (pivoting through grip safety).
10. Grip the grip safety in the left hand, and push up the mainspring housing into place, taking care to get the hammer strut pin correctly seated.
11. Replace mainspring housing pin.

To strip the firing pin and extractor from the slide.
1. Push firing pin in with a nail or match, and slide off the firing pin stop.
2. Remove firing pin and spring.
3. Pull out extractor from end of slide.

To re-assemble.
1. Replace extractor.
2. Replace firing pin and spring.
3. Press down the firing pin, and slide the firing pin stop (with stop to the left) into place.

HOW THE MECHANISM WORKS.

1. How the cartridges are fed up from the magazine into the chamber.

The first cartridge is brought up into the chamber from the loaded magazine by operating the slide with the left hand, while the right hand grips the butt of the pistol.

The fingers and thumb of the left hand grip the slide at the rear end by the roughened grips. The slide is drawn back. On releasing the slide, it is carried forward again by the recoil spring; and, coming forward, catches the rim of the top cartridge in the magazine and pushes it forward into the chamber.

2. How the hammer is cocked.

The backward motion of the slide cocks the hammer by rolling it back as it passes over it.

As the hammer rotates backwards the centre arm of the sear spring, pressing on the lower half of the sear, forces the sear, rotating on the sear pin, to engage in the bent of the hammer. The hammer is thus cocked. The hammer can also be cocked by hand. It can be placed at half cock or full cock.

The trigger is connected to the sear by the disconnector. The two are in connection when the disconnector is up, and out of connection when the disconnector is down.

When the disconnector is up, on pressing the trigger, the sear is released from the bent of the hammer; and the mainspring, operating on the hammer strut pin, throws the hammer forward, hitting the striker and firing the cap of the cartridge.

N.B. — (i.) The trigger cannot be pressed unless the grip safety is also pressed. This is done automatically by the grip of the hand on the butt. (ii.) The two other arms of the sear spring effect the return respectively of the trigger and grip safety.

3. **The automatic action.**

There are two forces which operate the pistol:

(i.) The backward force of the explosion of the cartridge;

(ii.) The forward force of the recoil spring.

The automatic operations of ejecting the empty cartridge, feeding a new cartridge into the chamber, and cocking the hammer are effected by the backward and forward motion of the slide.

The action of firing is done by the trigger working through the disconnector to the sear and hammer.

As soon as the cartridge is fired, the force of explosion, or recoil, drives the slide back. The barrel and slide are locked together by the projecting ribs on the upper side of the barrel engaging in the slots cut in the roof of the slide.

The slide recoiling thus carries the barrel with it; but the travel of the barrel is limited, since it is connected to the link which pivots on the slide catch. As the barrel recoils the link pulls the breech end of the barrel down; and so the slide and the barrel become disconnected.

The barrel then becomes stationary, while the slide, drawing the cartridge with it by means of the extractor, continues its backward motion, and ejects the cartridge.

This short recoil of the barrel ensures that the extraction of the cartridge will not commence until the bullet has left the muzzle, and so obviates loss of gas behind the bullet.

The slide, passing over the hammer, rotates it backwards and cocks it.

The slide is brought forward again by the recoil

spring; and a fresh cartridge is forced automatically into the chamber.

Before the slide has quite completed its forward travel, it comes in contact with a projection on the upper part of the breech end of the barrel. This causes the barrel to move forward with the slide, and the breech end, pivoted on the link, and slide catch to move upward, so that the ribs on the barrel become engaged again in the slots in the roof of the slide. The barrel and slide thus become locked together at the moment the slide has completed its forward travel.

N.B.—After firing the last round in the magazine the slide remains open.

4. The action of the disconnector.

The disconnector projects through the floor of the receiver, or body. It is forced up by the centre arm of the sear spring, pressing against its lower end.

There is a small recess cut in the under side of the slide, near the rear end. When the slide is fully forward this recess covers the disconnector, and so allows it to project up into the recess. At all other times, while the slide is moving backwards and forwards, it travels over the disconnector, thereby keeping it depressed.

As already explained in Section 2, "How the hammer is cocked," when the disconnector is up it connects the trigger to the sear, but when it is down it disconnects the two.

Thus the trigger cannot be pressed, and the hammer cannot fly forward, except when the slide is home.

COMPONENT PARTS OF THE ·455 WEBLEY-SCOTT AUTOMATIC PISTOL.

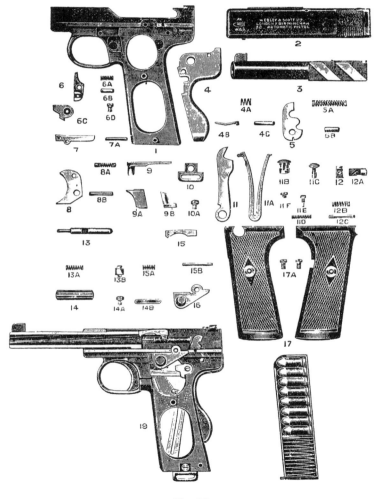

Fig. 22

DESCRIPTION OF COMPONENT PARTS.

1	Body.	11	Recoil Lever.
2	Breech.	11a	Recoil Spring.
3	Barrel.	11b	Recoil Lever Roller.
4	Safe.	11c	Recoil Lever Stop.
4a	Safe Spring.	11d	Recoil Lever Stop Spring.
4b	Holding Open Lever Spring.	11e	Recoil Lever Stop Screw.
4c	Safe Axis.	11f	Recoil Lever Roller Retaining Screw.
5	Hammer.	12	Magazine Bolt.
5a	Hammer Spring and Plunger.	12a	Magazine Bolt Thumb Piece.
5b	Hammer Axis.	12b	Magazine Bolt Spring.
6	Sear.	12c	Magazine Bolt Retaining Pin.
6a	Sear Spring.	13	Striker.
6b	Sear Axis.	13a	Striker Spring.
6c	Sear Tail.	13b	Striker Retaining Piece.
6d	Sear Screw.	14	Back Sight.
7	Holding Open Lever.	14a	Back Sight Screw.
7a	Holding Open Lever Axis.	14b	Back Sight Spring.
8	Trigger.	15	Extractor.
8a	Trigger Spring and Plungers.	15a	Extractor Spring.
8b	Trigger Axis.	15b	Extractor Axis.
9	Trigger Auxiliary Lever.	16	Breech Releasing Piece.
9a	Trigger Auxiliary Lever Cover Plate.	17	Stock.
9b	Trigger Auxiliary Lever Tripping Lever.	17a	Stock Screws.
10	Swivel.	18	Magazine.
10a	Swivel Screw.	19	Section of Pistol.

The Mechanism of the ·455 Webley-Scott.

How to strip the pistol.

Hold the pistol with the muzzle to the right, butt towards the body, forefinger of the right hand hooked into the trigger guard, and thumb of the right hand pressing on the lever stop (behind the trigger guard). With the left hand draw back the breech a short way, until the lever stop under the right thumb springs in. Then let the breech go forward again.

Now pull out the recoil lever bar and breech stop (on the right side of the pistol) as far as it will go.

Pull the breech right back.

Lift out the barrel.

Press down breech releasing lever (on left side of pistol); and slide the breech forward off the body.

To assemble the pistol.

Replace the breech and draw it back to its farthest position.

Replace the barrel.

Depress the breech releasing lever; and slide the breech forward.

Push in the recoil lever bar and breech stop.

Pull the breech a short way back, until the lever stop clicks out.

Let breech go forward again, and the pistol is reassembled.

The ·455 Webley-Scott.

The action of the mechanism.

There are two forces which operate the pistol:

(i.) The backward force of the explosion of the cartridge;

(ii.) The forward force of the recoil spring.

The automatic operations of ejecting the empty cartridge and feeding a new cartridge into the chamber and cocking the hammer are effected by the backward and forward motions of the breech.

The action of firing is done by the trigger working on the sear and hammer.

As soon as the cartridge is fired, the force of the explosion, or recoil, drives the breech back. The backward motion of the breech causes the barrel to travel back in a downward diagonal direction to the limit of the inclined grooves in the side of the body. This action ensures that the barrel and breech remain in contact; and the extraction of the cartridge does not commence until the bullet has left the muzzle.

The barrel, on reaching the limit of its travel in its inclined grooves, becomes stationary. The breech continues its backward motion against the force of the recoil spring, working through the recoil lever.

The breech passes over the hammer, rotating it backwards, and thereby cocking it.

The recoil spring and lever carry the breech forward again after the force of recoil is expended; and the breech, coming in contact with the base of the topmost cartridge in the magazine, pushes the cartridge forward into the chamber.

Just before the breech is fully home, the face of the breech comes in contact with the rear end of the barrel. Thus the breech carries the barrel forward with it, and causes it to travel forward and upward, until the breech and barrel go fully home and become locked.

The pistol is thus ready to fire on pressing the automatic grip safety and releasing the trigger.

Notes.

1. The breech remains back and open after the last cartridge in the magazine is fired.
2. The action of inserting a freshly loaded magazine automatically releases the breech, which flies forward and carries the first cartridge from the magazine into the chamber. This is a decided advantage over other pistols, in which the breech is not released automatically, but by an independent action of the hand operating the breech releasing lever.

CHAPTER X.

CARE AND CLEANING.

Wear in the bore of a firearm is due to:—
  (a) Friction of the bullet;
  (b) Heat from the gases;
  (c) Neglect of cleaning.

The first two causes are unavoidable; but a pistol, if well looked after, will fire many thousands of rounds before it becomes worn out. Neglect of cleaning, however, will soon spoil a pistol. When the weapon is new the bore has a bright polish; and this polish is a great safeguard from rusting and pitting. You should do all you can to maintain this polish, although it will, of course, gradually diminish with constant firing.

The pistol barrel is easier to clean than the rifle barrel, because it does not get so hot. When the barrel gets hot the metal expands, and the burnt gases get forced into the pores of the metal. After firing, these harmful products of the gases sweat out gradually; and, having a tendency to absorb moisture readily, they soon cause red rust to form if they are allowed to remain.

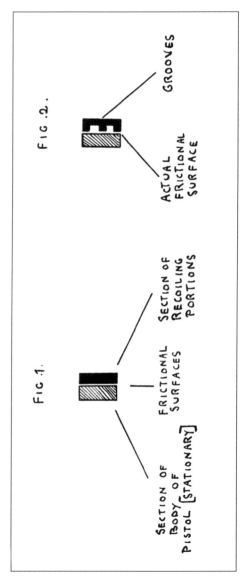

FIG. 1.

FIG. 2.

GROOVES

ACTUAL
FRICTIONAL
SURFACE

SECTION OF
RECOILING
PORTIONS

FRICTIONAL
SURFACES

SECTION OF
BODY OF
PISTOL [STATIONARY]

Fig. 23.— Diagram showing how the area of the frictional surfaces may be reduced by cupping and grooving. The grooves act as oil reservoirs and receptacles for grit and dirt that might otherwise obstruct the frictional surfaces.

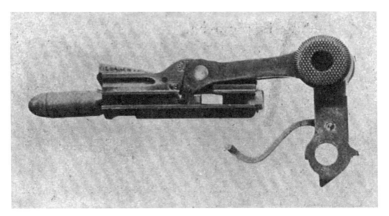

Fig. 24.—The Bolt of the Parabellum Pistol.

Note.—1. Grooves in the frictional surfaces.
      2. When there is a cartridge in the chamber the extractor
      projects and exposes the word "Geladen" ("Cocked").

Sweating is not so great in a pistol as in a rifle; but, still, it does exist, and must be watched for. The best way to remove this kind of fouling is by boiling water. Strip the pistol; and pour boiling water down the barrel by means of a funnel. The heat expands the metal; and the water washes the fouling out of the pores. Be very careful to dry the barrel completely after using the water.

After firing, the correct procedure for cleaning is this:—

1. Remove the superficial fouling, i.e., particles of burnt powder, with a dry rag and cleaning rod.
2. Clean out with tightly fitting oily rag (or strip pistol and use boiling water).

3. Pass dry clean rag through till no more fouling is removed.

4. Oil the bore, and clean all working parts with oily rag.

This procedure should be repeated for three days after firing.

Points to be observed in cleaning.

1. A wooden cleaning rod is preferable to a metal one, because the metal one frequently rubs the sides of the barrel, and, in time, wears a slight groove, causing inaccurate shooting.

2. The outside of the pistol should be slightly oiled, to prevent rust forming from the moisture of the hand.

3. Before firing always wipe out the barrel dry of oil.

4. Pay particular attention to removing dirt from:—

    (i.) The magazine (see that no dirt lies under the magazine platform);

    (ii.) Recoiling portions and slide;

    (iii.) All frictional surfaces;

    (iv.) The firing pin.

5. Strip the pistol occasionally for a thorough cleaning. Do not strip the pistol too often.

6. Clean immediately after firing—never delay.

7. To inspect the bore of the pistol, place your finger nail or a small piece of paper at the breech end at an angle to the line of the barrel, to reflect the light, and look down the muzzle end.

8. Never, on any account, use Globe Polish or emery powder to clean the bore. Use only rifle cleaning oil.

9. Nickelling can be removed by the use of Mottee Paste.

10. A good preventative of rust and fouling is B.S.A. Saftipaste. If the barrel is cleaned with this preparation after firing, no fouling will ever occur. It should be used by every pistol shooter.

11. In dry, sandy, or dusty countries, very little oil should be kept in the working parts of the pistol; and only thin oil should be used. Sometimes the automatic will work without oil, but it is not good for it.

12. The working parts normally must be well oiled.

Notes on the care of pistols.

1. Always keep the pistol in the holster. Be careful that the holster is dry. When putting a pistol away permanently, it is better to wrap it up in an oily rag, and put it in a box, and not leave it in a leather holster, otherwise it will be liable to rust.

2. Never put away a pistol in a case or holster leaving the hammer cocked or the firing pin spring compressed.

3. A little leather hammer protector should be improvised for all snapping exercises with an empty pistol. **Prove your pistol every time you draw it from the holster.**

CHAPTER XI.

PISTOL RANGES AND TARGETS.

Pistol ranges can be elaborate or simple. Even the poorest of ranges, however, should be equipped with a certain amount of apparatus for snapshooting, traversing and advancing targets. The following suggestions may be a help to anyone in designing a range, and in constructing apparatus for targets.

The Range.

The range should be on level ground and drained. If siting the range on the side of a hill, care should be taken to avoid "valleys" or folds in the ground down which water will drain. The best materials for the floor of the range are cinders and ashes. Sand is also good. The stop butt should be as high as possible; twenty feet is a good height; and the butt should have wings to catch stray bullets when firing at a crossing target.

The length of the range may usefully be fifty yards, to allow of advancing targets being used. Long range shooting can be practised best on the snapshooting range in the open, a description of which will follow. The breadth of twenty yards will allow a large number of people to fire, and will give a good run for the traversing target.

Well in front of the stop butt there should be a little wall, about 2ft. 6ins. high and 3ft. thick, built up on the floor of the range, in order to hide the disappearing targets, and protect the mechanism which works them. The wall of the parapet should be inclined on the firing point side at 30 degrees, and boarded and vertical on the target side.

On either side of the range, in line with this parapet, there should be made two protected shelters, or marker's butts, where the marker's sit and operate the moving targets. This arrangement is preferable to having wires and apparatus for working the targets from the firing point. The butts can easily be made with stakes and corrugated iron, or boards, with earth and sods piled against them to a thickness of three feet, to render them bullet proof. A roof should be provided, to prevent richochets from overhead wires, if these are used.

Portable firing tables should always be provided on the range.

It is useful to have an electric bell, to connect the firing point with the marker's butt, to signal the commencement and termination of practices, and to obviate the necessity for shouting or whistling. The bell wire should be overhead, at the side of the range, with bell pushes at 10, 15, 20, 25, 30 and 50 yards firing points.

Targets and Apparatus.

The stationary targets.

These should be 4ft. square, and made of 3in. by 2in. wood, covered with canvas, over which white paper is passed. The feet of the target should be 3ft. long, so making the total height 7 feet. By having big targets the damage to the woodwork is much less than with small targets, in which the wooden framework will soon get shot away. With a 4ft. square target only chance shots will hit the woodwork. The canvas can, of course, easily be renewed.

Flour paste or specially prepared paste known as "Tenaxis" will be needed, and also a supply of black and white patching paper. The central black aiming mark should be small, not bigger than 2ins. for 20 yards, or 4ins. for 50 yards shooting. There should be a black vertical line, 18ins. long, below the aiming mark, and reaching to within 2ins. of it.

A transparent celluloid grouping ring is useful for measuring the size of the shot groups.

Disappearing targets for snapshooting and rapid firing.

The mechanism for these is simply made by procuring a 4in. diameter scaffolding pole, and pivotting this on iron bearings at either end. The ends of the pole are bound by iron rings. The bearings, being pieces of 1/2in. iron rod, are driven into the pole for a distance of about 6ins., projecting 3ins.

One end of the pole reaches into the marker's butt, and has a crank handle 18ins. long bolted round it, by which it can be rotated by the marker.

Slots are cut in the pole to take iron fish plates, 2ins. broad, 6ins. long and 1/4in. thick. These fish plates are screwed to the wooden sticks, on to which the targets are nailed.

The targets themselves should be figure targets, representing the silhouette of a man's body.

If a very long pole is needed to carry, say, eight targets, or more, then two poles would be needed, and they would have to be joined together and a central roller bearing provided.

Traversing target.

The most satisfactory plan is to have light metal rails laid, and have a trolley on four wheels to carry the target. The trolley is pulled along by a rope wound up by drums three feet in diameter, worked by crank handles.

There should be two drums, one in either butt; one drum will wind the target one way and the other will wind it back again.

Don't Tug your Trigger.

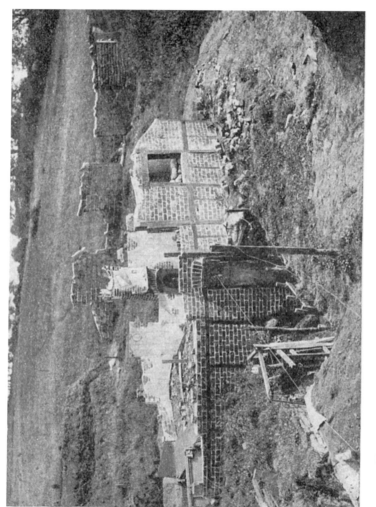

Fig. 25.—A pistol range constructed by the author while instructing officers in the army during the European War. Depth of range, 50 yards; width, 20 yards. The house and walls were made of painted canvas.

Fig. 26.—The range showing 11 disappearing relief model man targets exposed. The 12th target issued from doorway in foreground. The targets were operated by concealed wires.

The snapshooting range, with hidden targets.

The disadvantage of fixed targets on the ordinary range is that the firer knows the distance, the place where his target is coming up, and how long it will remain up. Much better practice is got by firing at targets that suddenly appear and disappear in places previously unknown to the firer. The targets should remain exposed for varying periods, some for four seconds and some for only one second. The targets should appear at a different range and in a different direction each time. Again, the target should be a realistic "man" target, in relief, and painted in natural colours. If one practises always at white paper targets with black "bull's-eyes", one will find it difficult to shoot quickly and accurately at a man's body. The two aiming marks are absolutely different.

The scheme for building the snapshooting range will, of course, vary with the amount of ground available, and the facilities for shooting in the open in any direction. Natural ground must be used if possible, and no artificial stop butts erected to spoil the natural aspect. The area could be anything up to 100 yards broad and 150 yards deep. Uneven ground with ditches, hedges, trees and old disused buildings afford good opportunities for hiding targets.

The firer can stand in one position, preferably on a platform about ten feet above the ground, so that he will be shooting down, and there will be less danger.

The targets provided may be heads or head and shoulders at close ranges, appearing and disappearing in windows of houses, over walls, behind hedges, or out of pits and ditches. At longer ranges full length figures can be arranged to appear round the sides of houses, in gaps in walls, from behind trees and bushes. Crossing and running targets can be worked on wires, or else by digging ditches and allowing a man to walk along the bottom of the ditch carrying the target on a pole above his head. This will be more lifelike, as it will reproduce the motion of walking or running.

The illustrations give different designs for target apparatus, all of which will be found easy to construct (but the measurements given must always be adhered to, in order to guarantee the working of the apparatus). Each different design has a different purpose. Thus, one provides for a target bobbing up and down vertically, while another gives the effect of a man looking round a corner, exposing his head and shoulders. Another design provides for a man target appearing in a doorway, exposing the whole of his body, etc., etc. Each design will have to be selected to suit the effect desired, and the shape of the ground where the target is to be placed.

The targets are operated by thin wires, which lie invisible on the ground; and they all lead to one protected shelter, where the marker sits and operates them. He can pull any wire he likes, or he can pull two together in different places. He is connected to the firing point by an electric bell or telephone. When the targets are cleverly placed in natural positions and the wires operating them are hidden the effect is very realistic

The construction of imitation houses, walls, etc.

Natural sized imitation houses can be easily erected out of wood and painted canvas. They look most effective with tumbled down walls standing from five to fifteen feet high, surrounded by piles of brick rubble and stones. Targets are arranged to appear in the windows; run across gaps in the walls; to appear out of the doors and run on wires.

A plan of the house must be made on the ground, and then timber posts driven into the ground at intervals of about three feet. Their height will depend upon the outline of the wall.

When walls are broken they must, of course, show "thickness," to resemble the real thickness of a wall, 9ins. or 12ins. The top edge of the wall can be made irregular by piling bricks or stones on it.

Canvas is stretched tightly over this wooden framework, and tacked down with large headed tacks. The canvas is prepared for painting by priming it with a coating of whitening mixed hot with boiled oil. The canvas will now take the paint well, and will stand the weather for a long time.

The construction of papier maché relief model targets.

These targets are easily made. They are very lifelike, and will last almost indefinitely, because they are patched up and repaired with the same material as they are made of. They will stand several hundred shots, and then become as good as new, if patched up and painted over again.

The half relief of a man's body or head and shoulders must be modelled first of all in clay. From the clay a plaster cast (negative) is made by pouring wet plaster over the model (a wooden frame, about 6ins. deep, holds the plaster round the sides of the model). Some strips of cheese cloth, or muslin, are mixed flat with the plaster, to strengthen it.

When the plaster sets hard the clay can be cut away, and a solid negative plaster mould remains.

Any number of papier maché impressions can be taken off the plaster mould by laying layers of paper soaked in paste, reinforced with glue. The first layer must be dry paper, so as not to stick to the plaster. The soaked paper is worked while soft into the shape of the mould with the fingers. Four or five layers of paper, with a final layer of linen or canvas, will be sufficient; and, when the whole dries, it can be lifted out of the plaster cast.

The paper relief target will dry quite hard and stiff if glue is used. Still greater hardness, approaching that of wood, can be obtained by coating the target with "resinite," made as follows: —

Heat three parts of carbolic acid crystals with four parts of formalin, adding also a little soda. Boil this for some time, and so obtain the yellow resinite solution which is used to saturate the paper of the target.

The target can then be painted in natural colours, and mounted on a wooden support to fit the target mechanism.

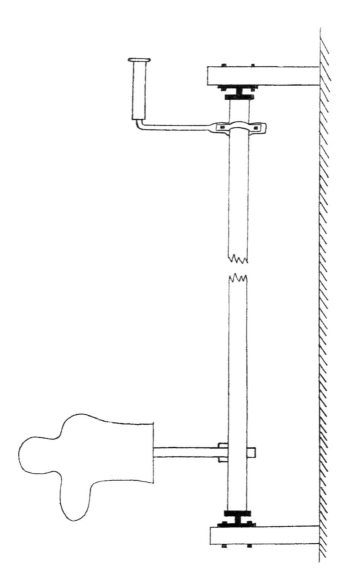

Fig. 27.—Apparatus for Snapshooting Targets.

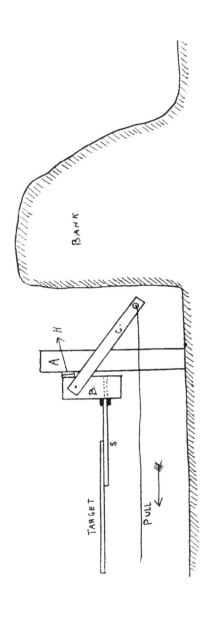

Fig. 28.—Apparatus for head and shoulder target appearing and disappearing behind bank or bush.

A.—4" x 4" post.

B.—4" x 4" block, hinged to A, 4" below top.

S.—Target support fits into slot in B 4" below hinge by means of an iron fish plate, and is removable.

C.—Lever arm.

Target drops of its own weight.

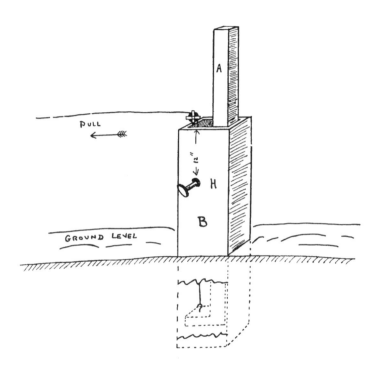

Fig. 29
Apparatus to give the effect of a target bobbing up behind a wall or out of a trench.

A.—Target support 2" x 2".
B.—Box, inside dimensions 2 1/2" x 4", in which A slides up and down.
H.—6" nail passing through hole in box B 12" below top. This nail checks upward rise of A. On removing nail, A can be removed.

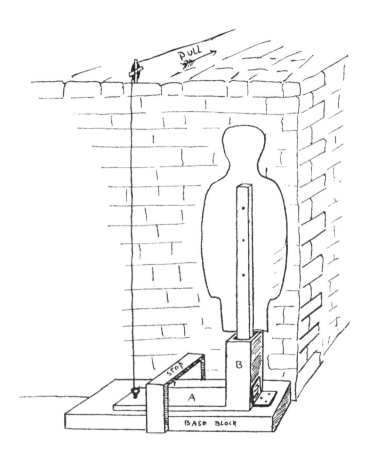

Fig. 30

Apparatus to give the effect of a man target looking round a corner exposing half of body.

A. — Lever arm.

B. — Box to hold target support (removable).

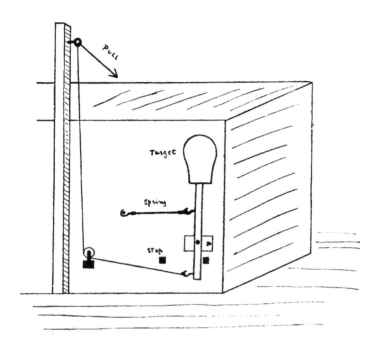

Fig. 31.
Apparatus to give the effect of a man's head looking round a corner.

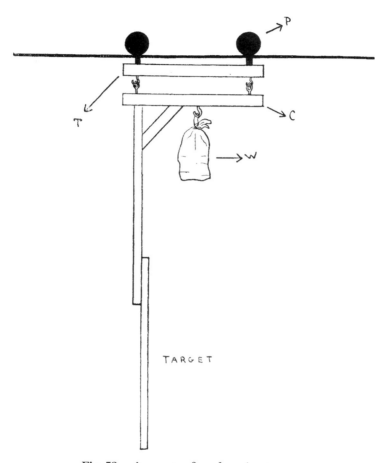

Fig. 32.—Apparatus for advancing targets.

T. Permanent trolley on overhead wire.
P. 2 1/2" pulley wheels.
C. Removable target carrier.
W. Weight (about 50lbs. earth in a sack) to ensure the steady run of target uninterrupted by winds.

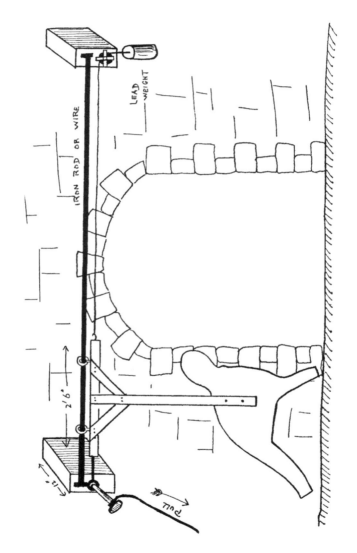

Fig. 33.—Apparatus for man target running across gap or doorway.

On releasing nail, weight pulls target across.

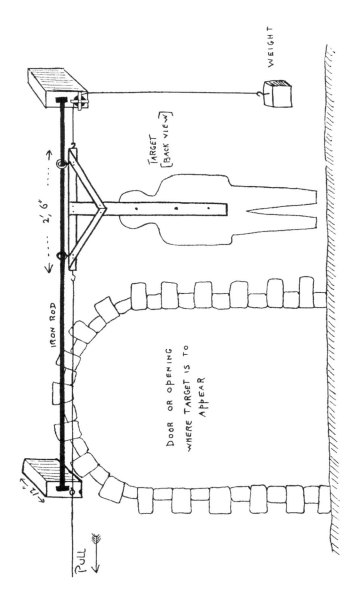

WEIGHT

TARGET [BACK VIEW]

2' 6"

IRON ROD

DOOR OR OPENING WHERE TARGET IS TO APPEAR

1½"

PULL

Fig. 34.—Apparatus for man target appearing and disappearing in doorway, exposing whole body.

CHAPTER XII.

THE MAXIMS OF PISTOL SHOOTING.

1. Prove your pistol every time you draw it from the holster.
2. Never hand over or accept a pistol unless proved.
3. The pistol is an ideal weapon for self defence.
4. Some people mistrust a pistol, because they have never learned how to use it.
5. Gain confidence in your pistol by learning how to use it, and finding out what you can do with it.
6. The pistol is a weapon of opportunity.
7. You seldom need a pistol, but when you do you need it mighty badly.
8. You cannot claim to be a pistol shot unless you are a quick shot.
9. Practise the correct handling of the pistol from the first; then you will handle it by instinct when the moment comes.
10. Shoot by sense of direction at close quarters.
11. Don't neglect your left hand.
12. Squeeze your trigger like you squeeze water from a sponge.
13. The timing of your trigger release just as your sights rise to the mark needs careful practice.
14. Trigger pressing is the secret of pistol shooting.
15. Pistol shooting is merely a matter of practice.
16. Don't hang on to the trigger. Release the finger fully after each shot.

17. Learn not to fumble. Practise a clean, quick action in drawing and handling your pistol.
18. Fire by sense of direction in the dark.
19. Fire fast in the dark.
20. Reload at the first opportunity. Always have a full magazine ready.
21. Change your pistol from right hand to left hand, according to the corner.
22. Keep cool. Fire fast, but never faster than "your best speed," or you will miss every time.
23. The art of quick shooting lies in perfection in the quick alignment of the sights, combined with an instinctive and automatic trigger squeeze.
21. If you are a good pistol shot, you will have nothing to fear from any man in the world.

J. B. L. NOEL.

BOOKS ON MUSKETRY, Etc.

PUBLISHED BY FORSTER GROOM & CO., LTD.

VISUAL TRAINING AND JUDGING DISTANCE.

By Captain J. H. SPIVEY. Post free, **1/1.**

THE DISCIPLINE OF MUSKETRY.

A Sequel to "The Theory of Musketry," which is reprinted with it. By Major O. ST. LEGER DAVIES, 6th Manchester Regt. Post free, **7d.**

MUSKETRY INSTRUCTION AND MINIATURE RANGE SHOOTING.

By Major D. McGREGOR JAMES, School of Musketry, Hythe. 3rd Revised Edition. Post free, **1/2.**

MILITARY LAW (corrected to date).

By Major T. KING (late Royal Berkshire Regiment). Post free, **2/9.** Chapter I on how to use the official handbooks is quite original, for no publication hitherto has touched upon this all-important feature.

INSTRUCTION ON THE LEWIS MACHINE GUN AND ITS HANDLING.

By SIMPLEX. A complete guide to the mechanism and tactical handling of the Lewis Automatic Machine Gun, and to the training of Machine Gun Sections. Post free, **2/8.**

VADE-MECUM FOR OFFICERS AND CIVILIANS PROCEEDING TO INDIA.

By Lieut. J. E. POWER, 19th Lancers (F.H.), Indian Army. Post free, **1/8.** The object in view is chiefly to guide those who may find themselves under orders for India, and are ignorant or in doubt as to what to take and not to take, how to go, and how to act at first as strangers in a strange land.

GUIDE TO COURTS MARTIAL DUTY.

By Major T. KING (late Royal Berkshire Regiment). Post free, **1/8.** This book is to assist officers in conducting the proceedings of courts martial. Details are given as to the Prosecutor and President regarding the various courts, the facilities and privileges that the accused is entitled to. They should be understood by all officers.

BATTALION MOVEMENTS IN THE ATTACK AT A GLANCE.

A brief description of the various formations assumed by an infantry Battalion in the successive stages of an attack—these formations being fully illustrated by a series of diagrams. A useful aid to Junior Officers and N.C.O.'s. By an ADJUTANT. Post free, **7d.**

AIMING AND FIRING.

The "Hythe" Method of Instructing Recruits, with a Note on Fire Discipline Training. By Captain H. WOOD HANBURY, 7th (D.C.O.) Middlesex Regiment. Post free, **10d.** The instruction given in this book has been written with a view of helping Musketry Instructors to standardise the teaching of their staff and consequently make it more efficient. The simplest language, suited to a recruit, has been used, and all unnecessary details omitted, while the Sequence of Instruction rigidly maintained throughout is that taught at Hythe.